C
H
I
N
E
S
E

ASTROLOGY

CHINESE ASTROLOGY

DECODE THE ZODIAC
TO LIVE YOUR BEST LIFE

MARITES ALLEN

MANDALA

CONTENTS

UNDERSTANDING
CHINESE ASTROLOGY

Astrology plays a significant role in Chinese philosophy and culture. In a generic sense, astrology is the study of the positions and movement of stars and planets and how they influence life on Earth and the specific behavior and destiny of its people. Compared to its Western counterpart, Chinese astrology has a deeper and richer context and complex features.

The origins of Chinese astrology are largely based on oral rather than written accounts; thus, elements vary depending on the source being used. Although much information has been lost, it is believed that this ancient system dates back more than four thousand years. It took hold during the Zhou dynasty (1046–256 BCE) and flourished during the Han dynasty (second century BCE to second century CE), with the introduction of the twelve zodiac animal signs.

Chinese astrology is deeply rooted in the philosophy of finding balance and harmony between human beings, society, and the universe to which they belong. This interaction between man and nature forms the basis of actions that lead to improving human life. This astrological field has many aspects, including the five elements theory, the yin and yang principle, the lunar calendar, and the Four Pillars of Destiny—all of which are discussed on the following pages.

In China, astrological consultations are mainly used for important life events, including the ideal dates for giving birth, getting married, and burials. Other common applications include using astrological signs to find compatible business or life partners, employees, and choosing ideal careers. The practice correlates a person's inherent traits with the ways in which they connect with others and the society in which they live.

Chinese astrology has influenced other zodiac systems, especially those in Asian countries that were once under the influence of China. While these zodiac systems are generally the same, some differences exist, such as stories of origin and featured animals. In modern cultures, other uses for the Chinese zodiac signs have emerged. It is now common to see related symbols being used for home decor, business logos, and body tattoos, for example. As such, they contribute to the ways in which cultures associate modern life with ancient beliefs.

THE FIVE ELEMENTS OF THE CHINESE ZODIAC

Feng shui is an ancient science that has its roots in the Chinese philosophy that all things on Earth are categorized into five basic elements—wood, fire, earth, metal, and water. Every element invokes a different mood, but too much or too little of each could lead to unwanted results.

WOOD symbolizes warmth, elegance, sensitivity, and generosity. Too much wood can be overwhelming and make a person stubborn and inflexible; too little, on the other hand, may manifest in depression, indecisiveness, and lack of growth.

FIRE symbolizes energy, innovativeness, and joy. Excessive fire can cause anger, aggression, irritability, and shortness of temper; whereas too little can lead to apathy, short-sightedness, and a lack of self-esteem.

EARTH symbolizes honesty, prudence, and hard work. When there is too much earth in a room, residents could feel heavy and bored, sluggish, and lack humor. Too little earth can make them lose focus and feel disorganized.

METAL symbolizes independence, ambition, and strength. If there is too much metal in a room, a person may turn out to be overly harsh and impulsive with their words and actions. When there is too little metal, a person may become too withdrawn or unreasonably cautious.

WATER symbolizes flexibility, diplomacy, kindness, and persuasiveness. Too much water can make a person too social for comfort or figuratively drowning in their emotions. Inversely, too little water can make a person feel stressed, isolated, and lonely.

Everything around us embodies the five elements. In order to create balance and harmony in your home or workplace, the key is to include furnishings and ornaments that represent all of the five elements in roughly equal measure. Placing relevant items in specific areas of the home or office intensifies their effect. For example, to activate the wood element, you might paint a room to the east or southeast of your home green.

	Wood	Fire	Earth	Metal	Water
Shape	Rectangular ▬	Triangular ▲	Square ◼	Round ●	Wavy 〰
Color	Green, light green	Red, pink, orange	Yellow, brown	White, gray, silver	Blue, black
Directions represented	↘ → Southeast, east	↓ South	↙ ↗ Southwest, northeast	← ↖ West, northwest	↑ North
Sample objects	Wooden furniture, fresh flowers, plants/ trees, natural fabrics	Light bulbs, sunlight, candles, electronic equipment	Landscape paintings, earth-toned draperies	Rocks/ stones, objects made of iron or aluminum	Mirrors, water features (fountains, aquariums)

YIN AND YANG

The concept of the five elements is closely associated with the principle of yin and yang. Both principles lend substance to the belief in the cycle of change—of being and ceasing to be; of beginnings and endings; of life, death, and rebirth—that rule natural and human events.

The concept of yin and yang dates back to the third century BCE, with the cosmologist Zou Yan as its principal proponent. Its roots go back further than this, however, as the concept also has associations with the c. eleventh-century BCE text known as *I Ching* or *Book of Changes*, which expressed that the continuously changing relationship between two opposite and complementing phenomena is responsible for the equally changing state of the universe and life as a whole.

Yin-yang refers to the duality or sets of opposing and complementing cosmic energies that govern the universe. Generally speaking, yin is the inner energy that is characterized as feminine, dark, passive, and negative. Yang, on the other hand, is the outward energy that is masculine, bright, active, and positive.

ATTRIBUTES AND ASSOCIATIONS

Yin-yang is a complex concept that, when interpreted or applied in daily affairs, maintains these basic truths: ① It is a consistent and logical pattern that can be seen in nature and in man; ② it represents changes in human nature that are similar to the waxing and waning of the moon; and ③ it is a process that ensures constant balance and harmony in all beings and circumstances.

Although the origins of the yin and yang symbol and the person who created it are unclear, the symbol as we know it today illustrates that each half of the circle has an element of the other (represented by the small dots). Each half complements the other, and an increase in one corresponds to a decrease in the other. The symbol is a representation of perfect balance.

Yin-yang is a cosmic reminder that there is a natural order to the universe and in human existence. Maintaining harmony is key because when this harmony is broken, or when there is great imbalance between the two qualities, problems, diseases, and even catastrophic events can occur.

YIN	YANG
Black	White
Moon	Sun
North	South
Earth	Heaven
Cold	Warm
Soft	Hard
Old	Young
Even numbers	Odd numbers
Rest	Activity
Winter	Summer

THE LUNAR CALENDAR

Unlike the widely used Western or Gregorian calendar, the Chinese lunar calendar starts the year somewhere between late January and early February, depending on the cycles of the moon. This timekeeping system counts the moon cycles from one lunar new year (spring season) to the next. It is also cyclical, meaning it is repeated time after time according to a pattern.

The lunar calendar reflects a sexagenary, or sixty-year, cycle. The cycle is based on the combination of ten Heavenly Stems and twelve Earthly Branches—a system that had its origins c. 2700 BCE when the ruling Yellow Emperor Huang Ti ordered a study of the changes between earth and sky, and the shifts in the four seasons to become the basis for the order of the cycle. The result was the sixty-year calendar where each year is represented by two characters: one Heavenly Stem and one Earthly Branch.

The Heavenly Stem is formed by combining one of the five elements (wood, fire, earth, metal, and water) with either yang or yin energy. The Earthly Branch is the corresponding Chinese zodiac sign for the given year. This stem–branch calendar is known in Chinese as *Jia Zi* (the start of a cycle). In ancient times, this sixty-year period represented a full lifespan, and people who live beyond this period and into the next *Jia Zi* are considered truly blessed. The current sixty-year cycle began in 1984, year of the wood Rat, and ends in 2043, year of the water Boar. The next cycle will then start in 2044, with another year of the wood Rat. (See also, The Four Pillars of Destiny, pages 19–21.)

Although the Western calendar is used in China for administrative purposes, the Chinese lunar calendar is used for setting traditional festivals and for timing agricultural activities in the countryside. Holiday celebrations, such as the Chinese New Year (see pages 198–203), the Lantern Festival, and Mid-Autumn Day are calculated based on the lunar calendar. This explains why the exact dates of the holidays vary each year. The lunar calendar is also popularly used to choose auspicious dates and times for important life events, such as a wedding, starting a business, house relocation, medical procedures, and so on.

DECODING YOUR ZODIAC SIGN

Each year in the Chinese lunar calendar represents a specific zodiac sign. Unlike the Gregorian year that starts unchangingly from January 1 to December 31, the lunar calendar varies each year and may start on any day in January or February. Thus, it will be easy for those born between March and December to figure out their zodiac sign. However, those born in January or February should use their exact dates of birth and refer to the chart on the following pages to identify their Chinese animal sign.

CHINESE ZODIAC YEARS FROM 1960 TO 2043

Year	Date	Chinese Zodiac Year
1960	January 28, 1960 – February 14, 1961	Rat
1961	February 15, 1961 – February 4, 1962	Ox
1962	February 5, 1962 – January 24, 1963	Tiger
1963	January 25, 1963 – February 12, 1964	Rabbit
1964	February 13, 1964 – February 1, 1965	Dragon
1965	February 2, 1965 – January 20, 1966	Snake
1966	January 21, 1966 – February 8, 1967	Horse
1967	February 9, 1967 – January 30, 1968	Sheep
1968	January 30, 1968 – February 16, 1969	Monkey
1969	February 17, 1969 – February 5, 1970	Rooster
1970	February 6, 1970 – January 26, 1971	Dog
1971	January 27, 1971 – February 14, 1972	Boar
1972	February 15, 1972 – February 2, 1973	Rat
1973	February 3, 1973 – January 22, 1974	Ox
1974	January 23, 1974 – February 10, 1975	Tiger
1975	February 11, 1975 – January 30, 1976	Rabbit
1976	January 31, 1976 – February 17, 1977	Dragon
1977	February 18, 1977 – February 6, 1978	Snake
1978	February 7, 1978 – January 27, 1979	Horse
1979	January 28, 1979 – February 15, 1980	Sheep
1980	February 16, 1980 – February 4, 1981	Monkey
1981	February 5, 1981 – January 24, 1982	Rooster
1982	January 25, 1982 – February 12, 1983	Dog
1983	February 13, 1983 – February 1, 1984	Boar
1984	February 2, 1984 – February 19, 1985	Rat
1985	February 19, 1985 – February 8, 1986	Ox

1986	February 9, 1986 – January 28, 1987	Tiger
1987	January 29, 1987 – February 16, 1988	Rabbit
1988	February 17, 1988 – February 5, 1989	Dragon
1989	February 6, 1989 – January 26, 1990	Snake
1990	January 27, 1990 – February 14, 1991	Horse
1991	February 15, 1991 – February 3, 1992	Sheep
1992	February 4, 1992 – January 22, 1993	Monkey
1993	January 23, 1993 – February 9, 1994	Rooster
1994	February 10, 1994 – January 30, 1995	Dog
1995	January 30, 1995 – February 18, 1996	Boar
1996	February 19, 1996 – February 6, 1997	Rat
1997	February 7, 1997 – January 27, 1998	Ox
1998	January 28, 1998 – February 15, 1999	Tiger
1999	February 16, 1999 – February 4, 2000	Rabbit
2000	February 5, 2000 – January 23, 2001	Dragon
2001	January 24, 2001 – February 11, 2002	Snake
2002	February 12, 2002 – January 31, 2003	Horse
2003	February 1, 2003 – January 21, 2004	Sheep
2004	January 22, 2004 – February 8, 2005	Monkey
2005	February 9, 2005 – January 28, 2006	Rooster
2006	January 29, 2006 – February 17, 2007	Dog
2007	February 17, 2007 – February 6, 2008	Boar
2008	February 7, 2008 – January 25, 2009	Rat
2009	January 26, 2009 – February 13, 2010	Ox
2010	February 14, 2010 – February 2, 2011	Tiger
2011	February 3, 2011 – January 22, 2012	Rabbit
2012	January 23, 2012 – February 9, 2013	Dragon
2013	February 10, 2013 – January 30, 2014	Snake
2014	January 31, 2014 – February 18, 2015	Horse

2015	February 19, 2015 – February 7, 2016	Sheep
2016	February 8, 2016 – January 27, 2017	Monkey
2017	January 28, 2017 – February 15, 2018	Rooster
2018	February 16, 2018 – February 4, 2019	Dog
2019	February 4, 2019 – January 24, 2020	Boar
2020	January 25, 2020 – February 11, 2021	Rat
2021	February 12, 2021 – January 31, 2022	Ox
2022	February 1, 2022 – January 21, 2023	Tiger
2023	January 22, 2023 – February 9, 2024	Rabbit
2024	February 10, 2024 – January 28, 2025	Dragon
2025	January 29, 2025 – February 16, 2026	Snake
2026	February 17, 2026 – February 5, 2027	Horse
2027	February 6, 2027 – January 25, 2028	Sheep
2028	January 26, 2028 – February 12, 2029	Monkey
2029	February 13, 2029 – February 2, 2030	Rooster
2030	February 3, 2030 – January 22, 2031	Dog
2031	January 22, 2031 – February 10, 2032	Boar
2032	February 11, 2032 – January 30, 2033	Rat
2033	January 31, 2033 – February 18, 2034	Ox
2034	February 19, 2034 – February 7, 2035	Tiger
2035	February 8, 2035 – January 27, 2036	Rabbit
2036	January 28, 2036 – February 14, 2037	Dragon
2037	February 15, 2037 – February 3, 2038	Snake
2038	February 4, 2038 – January 23, 2039	Horse
2039	January 24, 2039 – February 11, 2040	Sheep
2040	February 12, 2040 – January 31, 2041	Monkey
2041	February 1, 2041 – January 21, 2042	Rooster
2042	January 22, 2042 – February 9, 2043	Dog
2043	February 10, 2043 – January 29, 2044	Boar

FENG SHUI ASSOCIATIONS

The years of birth are associated with the duality of yin (an odd number at the end of a Gregorian calendar year) and yang (an even number at the end of a Gregorian calendar year) and the five elements, as follows:

GREGORIAN YEAR				
ENDS IN 0	**ENDS IN 1**	**ENDS IN 2**	**ENDS IN 3**	**ENDS IN 4**
YANG METAL	YIN METAL	YANG WATER	YIN WATER	YANG WOOD
ENDS IN 5	**ENDS IN 6**	**ENDS IN 7**	**ENDS IN 8**	**ENDS IN 9**
YIN WOOD	YANG FIRE	YIN FIRE	YANG EARTH	YIN EARTH

Thus, a Rat person born in 1948 is characterized as a yang earth Rat; an Ox person born in 1949 is a yin earth Ox; a Tiger person born in 1950 is a yang metal Tiger, and so on down the line.

THE FOUR PILLARS
OF DESTINY

In Chinese astrology, specifically in the practice of feng shui, there is a more sophisticated way of forecasting destiny using not just your birth year, but also the date and time of year. The system is called the Four Pillars of Destiny (or *BaZi* in Chinese) and follows a cosmic energy chart based on an analysis of your birth details and their relationship with changing cycles of energy, seasons, years, months, days, and even hours.

The Four Pillars provide not only insights into your strengths, weaknesses, and dominant character traits, but also help to analyze your prospects for luck at different life periods. Since interpreting the relation of the eight characters in a *BaZi* chart can be very complicated, an evaluation of your own chart is best done by a qualified feng shui consultant. They will adapt the necessary feng shui intervention to suit your specific needs.

HOUR	DAY	MONTH	YEAR
HEAVENLY STEM	HEAVENLY STEM	HEAVENLY STEM	HEAVENLY STEM
Yang Metal	Yin Metal	Yin Wood	Yin Water
EARTHLY BRANCH	EARTHLY BRANCH	EARTHLY BRANCH	EARTHLY BRANCH
Yang Rat	Yin Boar	Yin Ox	Yin Boar

↑ AN EXAMPLE OF A FOUR PILLARS, OR *BAZI*, CHART.

You may generate your own free personal destiny chart by visiting https://maritesallen.com/destiny-chart

The Four Pillars represent the year, month, day, and hour of your birth. Each pillar has two elements: one Heavenly Stem (the associated element combined with positive yang energy or negative yin energy) and one Earthly Branch (based on the Chinese zodiac signs). The combination of stem and branch in each pillar may be in harmony or they may clash. Harmonious combinations indicate a favorable prospect for the person, while clashing combinations indicate unfavorable prospects.

THE YEAR PILLAR   The Year Pillar represents ancestors and parents who govern your fortune from the age of 1 to 16. A favorable element indicates love by ancestors and blessings within the first sixteen years of your life. An unfavorable element may mean an unhappy childhood and possible family traumas. The Year Pillar represents characteristics that you are likely to share with people born in the same year.

THE MONTH PILLAR   The Month Pillar represents the typical inner qualities that are rooted in your older self. These characteristics may become more apparent in later years. In *BaZi* readings, this pillar represents your fortune from the age of 17 to 32 and reflects your relationships with parents and siblings. A lucky Month Pillar indicates parents with successful careers. An unlucky Month Pillar may point to parents who may not be able to provide adequate support.

THE DAY PILLAR   The Day Pillar represents the day-to-day persona that emerges in your social interactions with others. The characteristics that manifest in this pillar become dominant during the prime years of your life. In *BaZi*, this pillar represents your fortune from the age of 33 to 48, as well as experiences in middle age, including marital relationships. A favorable Day Pillar represents a successful career and happy marriage, while an unfavorable one indicates less than ideal situations.

THE HOUR PILLAR   The Hour Pillar represents innate characteristics that you prefer to hide for fear of being regarded as shallow. These qualities may come out at times when you are comfortable in the company of others, or during stressful situations. In *BaZi*, the Hour Pillar represents your offspring and your fortune from the age of 48 to 60. A favorable Hour Pillar represents obedient children, a meaningful career, and quiet years after retirement. An unfavorable Hour Pillar may bring rebellious children and other unfortunate events during your later years.

A Four Pillars of Destiny chart may be considered a cosmic blueprint of your destiny or as possible events in four stages of your life. Although these events are predetermined, you can change them according to your will and the decisions you make. Such a chart helps you to understand yourself and your innate strengths or weaknesses. With that awareness comes the power to change predetermined paths and help you grow and develop as a person.

USING THIS BOOK

While interpreting a destiny, or *BaZi*, chart like the one on page 20 is beyond the scope of this book, we hope that by providing the basic principles of Chinese astrology, and by helping you understand important aspects of your zodiac sign, you will have a better appreciation of your strengths and use them to guide you in making important decisions and in going about your daily activities.

Each chapter of this book takes a Chinese zodiac sign in turn and looks at the main personality types of a person born under that sign. Find out which animal relates to you and what this means in terms of your strengths, weaknesses, and for your prospects at work, in the home, in love, and in luck. You may yet discover a few things about yourself! You can also learn more about the characteristics of people who play important roles in your life. By knowing some of their traits, you can find ways to interact better with them, so finding harmony in all spheres of your life. Understanding past, present, and future indications in your life makes you less dependent on fate. Use the insight you gain in this book to manage phases in your life journey by exercising your free will and by making cautious decisions.

THE SIGNS

THE RAT

INTELLIGENT · OUTGOING · COOPERATIVE ·

26

THE OX

RELIABLE · HARDWORKING · DETERMINED ·

40

THE TIGER

CONFIDENT · TOLERANT · COURAGEOUS ·

54

THE RABBIT

SENSITIVE · AMIABLE · COMPASSIONATE ·

68

THE DRAGON

CHARMING · DECISIVE
· ENERGETIC ·

82

THE MONKEY

OPTIMISTIC · INVENTIVE
· CHARISMATIC ·

140

THE SNAKE

HUMOROUS · METHODICAL
· SYMPATHETIC ·

98

THE ROOSTER

CAPABLE · TRUTHFUL
· PHILOSOPHICAL ·

156

THE HORSE

SELF-SUFFICIENT
· GENEROUS · EASYGOING ·

112

THE DOG

LOYAL · LIVELY
· PERCEPTIVE ·

170

THE SHEEP

RESOURCEFUL · GENTLE
· CONSIDERATE ·

126

THE BOAR

HONEST · FORGIVING
· WELL-MANNERED ·

184

THE
RAT

I n Chinese culture, the Rat represents wisdom, wealth, and prosperity. It is said to have been the first to arrive when the Jade Emperor invited twelve animals to race for their place in the Chinese zodiac. Having won the race, the Rat starts the twelve-year astrology cycle.

RAT YEARS

1924, 1936, 1948, 1960, 1972, 1984, 1996, 2008, 2020, 2032

DATE RANGES FOR THE YEAR OF THE RAT

Start Date	End Date	Heavenly Stem	Earthly Branch
February 5, 1924	January 23, 1925	Wood	Water
January 24, 1936	February 10, 1937	Fire	Water
February 10, 1948	January 28, 1949	Earth	Water
January 28, 1960	February 14, 1961	Metal	Water
February 15, 1972	February 2, 1973	Water	Water
February 2, 1984	February 19, 1985	Wood	Water
February 19, 1996	February 6, 1997	Fire	Water
February 7, 2008	January 25, 2009	Earth	Water
January 25, 2020	February 11, 2021	Metal	Water
February 11, 2032	January 30, 2033	Water	Water

GENERAL
CHARACTERISTICS

As a Rat, you are an ambitious and creative type who is also likely to be a perfectionist. An experienced organizer, you are known for being able to handle even the most difficult problems. You work hard to achieve your goals, but can sometimes be unsure of yourself and might even prove unwilling to push your cause, which can be confusing.

Always fair in your conduct, you expect nothing less from those around you. Social interaction is your thing and no party is complete without your lively wit and humor. You are usually generous—with your attention as well as with your compliments—but those who impose on you should beware, for you value your privacy.

Your innate wisdom, coupled with a practical and sympathetic understanding of others, sees your peers constantly seeking your advice. You have a special way of dealing with crises and can come up with quick solutions to complex situations.

鼠

✳ RAT TYPES BY YEAR OF BIRTH

You will likely display one of five different personality types, based on your year of birth. The last number of your birth year determines your feng shui element, although you need to pay attention to the cutoff dates so you can determine your animal sign correctly. This is especially important if you were born in either January or February (see The Lunar Calendar, pages 12–13).

0 OR 1	↔	YOUR ELEMENT IS METAL	✛
2 OR 3	↔	YOUR ELEMENT IS WATER	🌊
4 OR 5	↔	YOUR ELEMENT IS WOOD	🌿
6 OR 7	↔	YOUR ELEMENT IS FIRE	🔥
8 OR 9	↔	YOUR ELEMENT IS EARTH	◈

WOOD RAT

1924 ▪ 1984

Yours is a friendly, outgoing personality that makes you popular with colleagues and friends. You have a quick mind and like to try your hand at anything you think may be useful. You have a great sense of humor, you enjoy travel, and, due to your highly imaginative nature, you are a gifted writer or artist. Your greatest fear is insecurity, but given your intelligence and capabilities, this fear is usually unfounded.

FIRE RAT

1936 ▪ 1996

Rarely still, you are possessed of boundless energy and enthusiasm.
You crave action, be it travel, following up new ideas, or campaigning
for a cause. An original thinker, you hate petty restrictions. Your
resilience is a credit to you and with the right support you can go far
in life. Forthright in your views, you are excitable and have a tendency
to commit yourself to undertakings without thinking
through all the implications.

EARTH RAT

1948 ▪ 2008

Astute and very levelheaded, you are not one to take unnecessary
chances. While you constantly try to improve your financial status,
you are prepared to proceed slowly and leave nothing to chance.
You are not the most adventurous type of Rat, preferring to
remain on familiar ground rather than take risks. You are talented,
conscientious, and caring toward loved ones, but can be
self-conscious and unduly worried about your image.

鼠

METAL RAT

1960 ▪ 2020

You have excellent taste and appreciate the finer things
in life. Your home is comfortable and beautifully decorated.
You thrive on entertaining and mixing in fashionable circles,
and are exceptionally loyal to family and friends. Financially astute,
you invest well. On the surface you are cheerful and confident,
but deep down you can be troubled by worries—all too often
of your own making.

WATER RAT

1932 ▪ 1972

Intelligent and astute, you are a deep thinker who expresses
your thoughts clearly and persuasively. You are always eager
to learn and have many talents. You are a particularly skillful writer,
but easily become sidetracked and have trouble concentrating
on just one thing at a time. Though you are popular, your fear
of loneliness sometimes leads you into the wrong company.

RAT TYPES BY MONTH OF BIRTH

Use the month of your birth to pinpoint your dominant personality type in a single word or phrase.

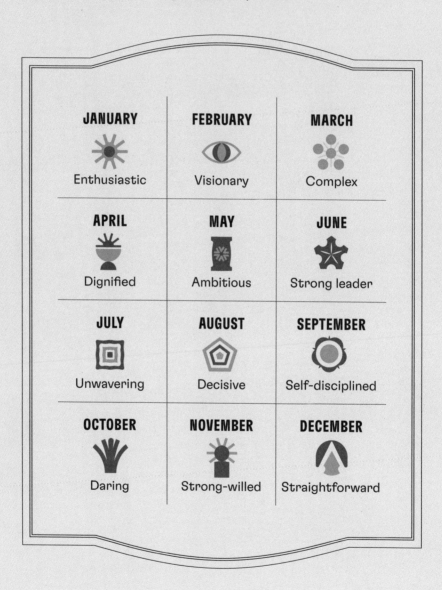

JANUARY	FEBRUARY	MARCH
Enthusiastic	Visionary	Complex
APRIL	**MAY**	**JUNE**
Dignified	Ambitious	Strong leader
JULY	**AUGUST**	**SEPTEMBER**
Unwavering	Decisive	Self-disciplined
OCTOBER	**NOVEMBER**	**DECEMBER**
Daring	Strong-willed	Straightforward

鼠

FENG SHUI ADVICE

Our luck indications change every year, every month, and every day, and the best way to plot this is through the use of a reliable feng shui almanac. The following information is meant as a general guide for the Rat.

	Lucky	Unlucky
Numbers	2, 3, 23, 32	5, 9, 59, 95
Days	3rd, 6th, 20th of the month Success day*: Wednesday Vitality day**: Tuesday	10th, 23rd, 26th of the month Unlucky day***: Saturday
Colors	Black, blue, gold, green	Red, pink, purple, yellow, brown
Directions	North, northwest, west, southwest	South, southeast
Flowers	Lily, primrose, African violet	

* SUCCESS DAY This day is filled with positive energy and is considered lucky when planning important personal activities or social events.

** VITALITY DAY This is the day when you are most active and vibrant.

*** UNLUCKY DAY This day is considered inauspicious and you should avoid it when planning important personal activities or social events.

FENG SHUI FACT

In Chinese culture, rats represent diligence and prudence; that is why many people born in a Rat year tend to be wealthy and prosperous. They also possess vitality, fertility, and a high survival rate; thus, the rat is considered a lucky symbol for couples hoping to conceive.

YOUR CHARACTER STRENGTHS

Anyone born in the year of the Rat is naturally very charming—you know it! Outgoing, cheerful, and sociable in character, you have plenty of friends because you get along with just about anybody.

You work hard to achieve your goals because you have superior standards in life, and wild ambition pushes you to put more effort into accomplishing whatever you set your mind on. And, of course, the hard work pays off—you are extremely successful. You have an innate intelligence that has a way of maximizing any opportunity you run into.

Perhaps your greatest strength is your incredible thirst for learning. It starts early in life, in childhood, and continues into your senior years. Highly disciplined, you like to gather and analyze information, a trait that never fails to enrich your life.

PERCEIVED WEAKNESSES

You are a stubborn type who rarely listens to advice from those around you. That outstanding instinct of yours makes you quick to criticize or complain, and you are picky about the shortcomings of others, which unwittingly causes offence. Vain and calculating, you like to boast about your achievements to attract more interest and attention, but unfortunately this often has the opposite effect, provoking resentment.

You need to be mindful of overstretching yourself, as you tend to cast your energy in multiple directions with only burnout to show for your efforts. This inability to focus, together with a lack of persistence or stability, makes you a frequent changer of jobs.

You may appear to be laid-back or relaxed, but beneath the surface you are restless, a little nervous even. The many friends you attract are not only there for your upbeat side, they would love to know all about you ... if only you would let them in.

DOMINANT STRENGTHS	DOMINANT WEAKNESSES
Intelligent	Materialistic
Responsible	Timid
Cooperative	Unpredictable
Adaptable	Stubborn
Cautious	Critical
Perceptive	Picky
Alert	Changeable
Positive	Demanding
Flexible	Self-centered
Outgoing	Boastful

PROSPECTS FOR
YOUR CAREER

As a Rat, you are hardworking, observant, and imaginative; you are ever full of ideas. Such characteristics make you an excellent candidate for a writer, human resources manager, or PR officer.

THE DAY-TO-DAY

In particular, you excel in sales and marketing roles. This is because you thrive in any job that calls for interaction and communication. But having a sociable personality does not stop simply at getting along with others, it is your *genius*. Used well, it can help you advance, improve, and reach your full potential. However, this social aspect of your personality can also be your downfall. Well aware of your capabilities, you are prone to overcommit. True, you will go far with your talents, just try not to bite off more than you can chew.

Also on the downside, you tend to falter in times of uncertainty, and if you are hesitant to promote your ideas or get bogged down in bureaucratic routine, you may find yourself missing chances of promotion. Ever the opportunist, you are in the habit of pouncing unthinkingly on money-making schemes that squander your energies. You can likewise be gullible and easily find yourself taking on too much and falling short. Concentrating on one thing at a time is the best route to success for you.

BUSINESS SENSE   In business, you are a great opportunist. You are good at goal setting, planning, and organizing activities. Charming and tactful, you keep your emotions under control, giving others the impression that you are always on top of things. But you are not one for lengthy discussions, neither are you great at sticking to one goal for any length of time. This should not dismay you, but should encourage you to seek healthy partnerships that enable you to play to your strengths—primarily handling personnel and office morale—while letting others handle the rest.

THE LONG GAME   No matter what jobs you pursue, you will always harvest success on account of your ability to adapt and to react positively to change. Bold and optimistic in your outlook, you face hardships and challenges with a calm demeanor, relying on your instinct to get you through. Disasters make your capabilities all the more outstanding. You will always do well in business as a result. Whatever path you choose, rest assured that you will not suffer any great losses or failures, and that you are likely to accomplish something later in life, around your fifties.

PROSPECTS FOR DOMESTIC LIFE

When it comes to family matters, you do everything you can to provide for, and please, your loved ones. Caring and thoughtful with family members and friends, you feel a great sense of responsiblity for their well-being. But take care not to become overprotective, as this can be counterproductive.

THE IDEAL HOME

A Rat's home is a safe place that protects residents from life's difficulties. Everything should be practical and easily accessible. The water element is essential for you, so fill your home with fountains, mirrors, and water-inspired paintings or decorations. Pay special attention in the bathroom, using the colors of blue and gold to achieve the necessary yin and yang balance. Above all, make sure your home has plenty of space—wide-open spaces because you are always on the move, and a large den-like space where family members can gather to learn new skills, musical instruments, and the like. And do not overlook secret hideaways! You may not be as brave as the other animal signs, but you are a born survivor. Although your home need not be a fortress, the odd safe nook is essential for those quiet moments of uncertainty and self-reflection.

FAMILY LIFE

Relationships between parents and children in your household should be fairly placid. Highly intuitive of the moods of your young ones, you rarely need help from books or child psychologists to get into the inner worlds of your offspring. Your sensitive and loving nature enables you to create perfect harmony and understanding in the family. You are not one to impose harsh discipline in your household—you prefer to win the respect of your children through love and trust, rather than fear. There is nothing you love more than to tell stories of your own childhood experiences and this serves as meaningful instruction and inspiration to your listeners. Have no doubt that your children will benefit from this.

FRIENDSHIP AND LOVE

Your optimistic nature makes you an attractive prospect for potential partners and you will always have plenty of admirers. Once settled, you may give the impression that you are careless, a little cowardly even, but deep down you are tender and delicate. You are extremely understanding and tolerant of the people you love.

BEST FRIENDS

Throughout your long and eventful life, you will make many friends, especially with fellow Rats, and those born under the signs of the Ox, the Dragon, and the Monkey. You also get along well with those born under the signs of the Tiger, the Snake, the Rooster, the Dog, and the Boar. Sensitive Rabbits and Sheep find you a bit too blunt for their liking, while Horses are just too unpredictable for your security-conscious needs.

LOVE MATCHES

Your perfect partner is your secret friend the Ox, who will be attracted to your passion and who will be faithful to your union. The Dragon shares your straightforward nature and need for personal space to be respected. A union with a Monkey can be harmonious and prosperous, and one in which you will continue to discover potential for each other. If you do not manage to find one of these three ideals, you may find acceptable matches with Tigers, who understand you and with whom there are no big quarrels. You may also find complementary matches with the reliable Rabbit, the romantic Dog, or the persistent Boar.

	RAT	DRAGON	MONKEY
FRIENDS AND ALLIES			

THE PERFECT MATCH — OX

The Ox is the second animal in the Chinese zodiac hierarchy. Owing to its animal characteristics of great strength and endurance, it has become a symbol of diligence, patience, and perseverance. It also has connotations of wealth and prosperity.

OX YEARS

1925, 1937, 1949, 1961, 1973, 1985, 1997, 2009, 2021, 2033

DATE RANGES FOR THE YEAR OF THE OX

Start Date	End Date	Heavenly Stem	Earthly Branch
January 24, 1925	February 12, 1926	Wood	Earth
February 11, 1937	January 30, 1938	Fire	Earth
January 29, 1949	February 16, 1950	Earth	Earth
February 15, 1961	February 4, 1962	Metal	Earth
February 3, 1973	January 22, 1974	Water	Earth
February 19, 1985	February 8, 1986	Wood	Earth
February 7, 1997	January 27, 1998	Fire	Earth
January 26, 2009	February 13, 2010	Earth	Earth
February 12, 2021	January 31, 2022	Metal	Earth
January 31, 2033	February 18, 2034	Water	Earth

GENERAL CHARACTERISTICS

Of all the signs in the Chinese zodiac, you are the one with the greatest strength and determination. You are incredibly patient, tireless in your work, and capable of enduring any amount of hardship without complaint. Such stability and persistence inspires confidence in others. You may not talk much, but when you do, what you have to say is intelligent, articulate, and eloquent. You have a logical mind and approach every task in a systematic way. Although you are not driven by the prospect of financial gain, you seem to gain wealth easily on account of your honesty.

Your quiet aura should not be mistaken for lack of inner strength. On the contrary, your sense of right or wrong will not tolerate unwarranted means to achieve your life goals. You have what it takes to be a good leader owing to your steadfastness and independence. Some may interpret this quality as being harsh, but to you it is simply dedicating yourself to the things you love in life. You rarely make a choice without careful thought, but once you start something, you will work on it nonstop and see it to completion.

✳ OX TYPES BY YEAR OF BIRTH

You will likely display one of five different personality types, based on your year of birth. The last number of your birth year determines your feng shui element, although you need to pay attention to the cutoff dates so you can determine your animal sign correctly. This is especially important if you were born in either January or February (see The Lunar Calendar, pages 12–13).

1 OR 2	↔	YOUR ELEMENT IS METAL	✛
3 OR 4	↔	YOUR ELEMENT IS WATER	🌊
5 OR 6	↔	YOUR ELEMENT IS WOOD	🌿
7 OR 8	↔	YOUR ELEMENT IS FIRE	🔥
9 OR 0	↔	YOUR ELEMENT IS EARTH	⬤

WOOD OX

1925 ▪ 1985

While a little on the conservative side, you remain open-minded to the ideas of others. You have a flexibility that promises great success in your chosen career, where you earn respect for your high morality and natural ability to work well with others. Beware of a readiness to flare your nostrils in anger when provoked, and try to avoid a tendency to be a little too honest when expressing your views.

FIRE OX

1937 ▪ 1997

You are the most assertive of all Ox types, are hardworking, and show true leadership potential. You have a strict, almost militant, approach to life, which sees you overcoming even the most challenging of situations. You can be stubborn and a little bossy, however, and others read this as arrogance. You need to be careful not to allow this to get in the way of making important decisions.

EARTH OX

1949 ▪ 2009

A rational type, you have a grounded outlook that is much appreciated by others. Well aware of your own strengths and weaknesses, you are not one to overcommit yourself. This makes you an influential team player and a relentless worker who can always be trusted to complete a task. You may not work as swiftly as others, but you do so efficiently and thoughtfully. Ever practical, if you have a fault, it is that you do not show your thoughts or emotions easily.

METAL OX

1961 ▪ 2021

Known and respected for your integrity, you make an exceptional partner or friend. You may not be the most demonstrative of people, but you can be trusted to take good care of your family. In the workplace, you may not appear to be a team player, but your drive and tireless energy see you through any project you set your mind to. Be careful though: once you are focused on a certain task, it can be difficult for others to divert your attention elsewhere and this can lead to grudges against you.

WATER OX

1973 ▪ 2033

For an Ox, you are refreshingly flexible, easygoing, and willing to incorporate changes into your system ... as long as they are not too radical. You are also more sociable than other Ox types and more open to other points of view. Ever patient and resilient, you are able to work most things through—both at work and in your personal life—in a characteristically quiet and unobtrusive way.

OX TYPES BY MONTH OF BIRTH

Use the month of your birth to pinpoint your dominant personality type in a single word or phrase.

JANUARY	FEBRUARY	MARCH
Creative	Temperamental	Unpredictable
APRIL	**MAY**	**JUNE**
Tenacious	Indecisive	Indefinite
JULY	**AUGUST**	**SEPTEMBER**
Bullheaded	Genial	Nimble
OCTOBER	**NOVEMBER**	**DECEMBER**
Frank	Organized	Flexible

牛

FENG SHUI ADVICE

Our luck indications change every year, every month, and every day and the best way to plot this is through the use of a reliable feng shui almanac. The following information is meant as a general guide for the Ox.

	Lucky	Unlucky
Numbers	1, 4, 14, 41	4, 9, 49, 94
Days	12th, 14th, 17th of the month Success day*: Saturday Vitality day**: Wednesday	18th of the month Unlucky day***: Thursday
Colors	Cream, beige, white, yellow	Green, blue
Directions	Northeast, north, south	Southwest
Flowers	Plum, cherry, peach blossom, tulip	

* SUCCESS DAY — This day is filled with positive energy and is considered lucky when planning important personal activities or social events.

** VITALITY DAY — This is the day when you are most active and vibrant.

*** UNLUCKY DAY — This day is considered inauspicious and you should avoid it when planning important personal activities or social events.

ZODIAC FACT

The Ox is one of only two animal symbols in the Chinese zodiac that also feature in Western astrology (the other is the Sheep). As the strongest animal among the twelve Chinese zodiac signs, it has a special significance in agriculture where it is considered the most important helper of humans.

YOUR CHARACTER STRENGTHS

You are a serene and driven individual, but your quiet aura does not indicate a lack of inner strength. On the contrary, you have a robust sense of right and wrong and will not tolerate unwarranted means to achieve your life goals.

You are not one to make any kind of decision without careful thought, but once you start something, you will work on it nonstop to see it through. This aspect of your personality can play to your advantage when pursuing a given career. Setting much store on your authenticity and independence, you will always insist on doing things your way rather than collapse under the pressure of accepting suggestions from others.

Naturally peaceful and levelheaded, you like to run things your own way, slow and steady. Take care here, however, as you tend to sulk if things do not go your way. Your incredible patience knows no bounds . . . almost. It is possible to push you too far and, once challenged or angered, you can be a fierce opponent. Locked horns and steaming nostrils are metaphors that spring to mind!

牛

PERCEIVED WEAKNESSES

You sometimes struggle to express your emotions or views to those around you. Some take this to mean that you are an introvert, but in all honesty you are simply showing your resolute Ox blood. You feel compelled to face difficulties alone, without help from others.

If you tend to lack humor, it is because you are practical and choose to communicate based on facts—you are not one to dabble in the fantasies of the whimsical world. Instead your focus is firmly on the reality of the ground you walk on.

A great consumer of knowledge, you like to learn new things, but this has its limits—once you are on a certain track it is difficult to persuade you to change direction. Because of this, you may find yourself sticking at something for too long, whether at work or in your personal life. Perhaps check in with yourself once in a while to make sure this aspect of your personality is not holding you back.

Beware of your natural tendency toward neatness and organization. This quirk also reveals you to be a stickler for punctuality and you find it difficult not to show your frustration when others are late for an engagement.

DOMINANT STRENGTHS	DOMINANT WEAKNESSES
Hardworking	Uncompromising
Reliable	Insecure
Honest	Solitary
Persistent	Stern
Levelheaded	Conservative
Strong-willed	Distant
Determined	Stubborn
Patient	Strict

PROSPECTS FOR YOUR CAREER

Given your steadfast nature, you find great value and meaning in a stable job that truly interests you. Once you find the ideal work situation, you strive to make the best of it.

PLAY TO YOUR STRENGTHS

With exceptional organizational skills and perseverance, you are bound to succeed in whatever career you choose. Among the types of jobs particularly suited to an Ox are those in the fields of agriculture, politics, and anything that requires expert studies. You might also find yourself excelling in a career in the arts.

Athough seemingly quiet in daily life, you can be sociable and practical and actually possess excellent communication skills. You are very good at expressing your thoughts and have no trouble getting along with others. If you use these strengths in the sales field, you will succeed and could even make a lot of money— you have persuasive skills that others lack.

Steady and self-dependent, you make a fine leader as you rarely seek help or advice from others. Some may see your methods as harsh, but actually they are an expression of your great sense of dedication to the things you love in life. In the long run, your working methods prove that you can be trusted to fulfill your commitments to submit work on time. Such dedication to the job earns you the respect and support of others, who admire the fact they can count on you.

COMMON PITFALLS

Be wary of falling into the trap of feeling underrated, of thinking your talents are wasted, or worrying about your superiors failing to notice your hard work and capabilities. Instead, try to work well with the higher-ups to make sure they notice your ability to get things done even in the most challenging of situations. In order to achieve this, you need to ditch a little of your stubbornness and establish good communication channels.

PROSPECTS FOR DOMESTIC LIFE

It is in your nature to be both predictable and traditional. Thus, in terms of loyalty and support, you do not disappoint—you will do just about anything to ensure the comfort and safety of your loved ones. When it comes to family life, however, your somewhat disciplinarian ways can cause friction.

PARENTING

You may not be very demonstrative, but there is no doubt that you are loving. You always provide and care for your children and they never lack for anything that money can buy. When it comes to discipline, however, try not to be too demanding. It is in your nature to want everything to be just so, but you can be a little too rigid for your own good. For example, you expect obedience and respect. You are not wrong in this, but to earn love at the same time, try to strike a balance where the respect is mutual. Sharing these values with your children will be a great source of joy to you.

HOME COMFORTS

In keeping with your character, your home is traditional and may even have a farmstead vibe. The decor is conservative and inviting, warm and comfortable as a result. You benefit from living in a house with big windows that let natural elements come flooding in. You do just fine without any flashy gadgetry, neither do you need spaces to hide secrets in—just a normal abode for quiet and comfortable living. Your furnishings are classic and robust—nothing too trendy or dependent on technology. Try to incorporate more earth element accents and fewer wood-inspired ones. Ceramic and porcelain fulfill the brief here—look for decorative bowls and fill them with colorful rocks and crystals.

牛

FRIENDSHIP AND LOVE

As a friend or lover, you may come across as reserved, but this impression changes and, with time, you reveal yourself to be sweet and caring. You are very dedicated to your friends and it is not unusual for a long-term friendship to develop into a romantic relationship.

COMPATIBILITY

The best friends and lovers for an Ox are the Rat, the Snake, and the Rooster. However, you can also have meaningful relationships with the Rabbit, the Dog, the Monkey, and another Ox. You find it hard to have a Sheep in your circle, though, as you have very little in common with this sign. The same can be said for the Dragon, the Horse, and the Tiger. Select friends—and especially lovers—carefully. You are naturally picky about who you like and this tends to take time. Once you find that special person, however, you do anything to win their affection. No other sign demonstrates such persistence in love.

LOVING AND LOYAL

When lucky in love, you adore your partner and are not the type to stray away. You may not be the best at expressing your feelings, but words are not always necessary. Your sincerity is often evident in your actions and you rarely fail to show your true intention. Be wary of a lack of romance, however, and look for ways to be more passionate; go out of your way to show you care. Conversely, anyone trying to win your attention will not impress you with fancy dates or expensive love tokens. No, you respond best to loyal and wholehearted commitment, pure and simple.

FRIENDS AND ALLIES	OX	SNAKE	ROOSTER
	🐂	🐍	🐓

THE PERFECT MATCH — RAT

THE
TIGER

The third animal sign in the Chinese zodiac is the Tiger, known widely throughout China as the king of all beasts. Fierce and mesmerizing, this animal is a popular symbol of bravery and strength.

TIGER YEARS

1926, 1938, 1950, 1962, 1974, 1986, 1998, 2010, 2022, 2034

DATE RANGES FOR THE YEAR OF THE TIGER

Start Date	End Date	Heavenly Stem	Earthly Branch
February 13, 1926	February 1, 1927	Fire	Wood
January 31, 1938	February 18, 1939	Earth	Wood
February 17, 1950	February 5, 1951	Metal	Wood
February 5, 1962	January 24, 1963	Water	Wood
January 23, 1974	February 10, 1975	Wood	Wood
February 9, 1986	January 28, 1987	Fire	Wood
January 28, 1998	February 15, 1999	Earth	Wood
February 14, 2010	February 2, 2011	Metal	Wood
February 1, 2022	January 21, 2023	Water	Wood
February 19, 2034	February 7, 2035	Wood	Wood

GENERAL
CHARACTERISTICS

You are a sensitive type who is given to deep
thinking and are capable of great sympathy.
A born leader, you are much admired for your
determination and boundless optimism. You have
a magnetic personality as well as a natural air
of authority—a combination that makes you
irresistible to others. You tend to be image
conscious and take good care of your reputation,
which is not that difficult given your popularity
with those who share your views.

Although you make a courageous and generous
friend, you are prone to being inflexible and self-
centered if you are not able to achieve what you
want. Your fiery nature can get you into trouble
at times—you have an extremely short temper,
for instance. Conversely you can sometimes be
hesitant, leading to poor or late decision-making.

Being aware of your strengths can make you too
confident and feel that you do not need much help
from others. You can be a potentially good leader,
if only you can handle negative feedback and not
take it against anyone who calls your action down.

TIGER TYPES BY YEAR OF BIRTH

You will likely display one of five different personality types, based on your year of birth. The last number of your birth year determines your feng shui element, although you need to pay attention to the cutoff dates so you can determine your animal sign correctly. This is especially important if you were born in either January or February (see The Lunar Calendar, pages 12–13).

0 OR 1	↔	YOUR ELEMENT IS METAL	✛
2 OR 3	↔	YOUR ELEMENT IS WATER	🌊
4 OR 5	↔	YOUR ELEMENT IS WOOD	🌿
6 OR 7	↔	YOUR ELEMENT IS FIRE	🔥
8 OR 9	↔	YOUR ELEMENT IS EARTH	✿

FIRE TIGER

1926 ▪ 1986

Full of energy, you are the type who leaves a lasting impression on those with whom you interact. Independent and capable, you do not like to turn your back on any challenge. You have quick reflexes and a keen sense of observation, which makes you a fast learner. You can be trusted to follow directions in a highly efficient manner. You possess enviable communication skills and, because of your eloquence, you can be very persuasive; you have no trouble rallying the support of others.

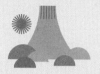

EARTH TIGER

1938 ▪ 1998

You have tremendous self-confidence and with good reason. Practical and sensible, you make decisions based on deliberate thought and refuse to be influenced by fanciful ideas that sound great but are difficult to implement. With your capacity for hard work and discipline, you can be very productive. You are capable of great learning and always apply this to achieve the best results. Having said that, you like to rely on what you know and are rarely persuaded to try new activities.

METAL TIGER

1950 ▪ 2010

Perhaps the most ambitious of all Tiger types, you have great drive and passion. Your level of energy is such that you stop at nothing to get things done—even if they are beyond your expectations. You do, however, have a tendency to focus more on your own interests than on those of others, and to achieve your goals regardless of the sentiments of those around you. This trait is not always taken lightly by others.

WATER TIGER

1962 ▪ 2022

Highly intelligent, you thrive in fields that involve human dynamics, such as teaching and hospitality. You are an excellent communicator who has no trouble rallying others to support noble causes. You are sensitive to the needs of others and make a good role model in pursuit of your own goals. You are open-minded and quite willing to try new ideas. Although you can be indecisive when faced with a challenging situation, you are persistent and do not give up easily.

WOOD TIGER

1934 ▪ 1974

A social animal, you do well in a host of different circles with varied interests, and enjoy great relationships, some of which can help you achieve your goals. You like to take things in moderation, which makes it easy for you to win the support of those around you. A born mediator, you can be trusted to protect weaker people from aggressive bullies. You look for the good in others and do not think negatively of anyone without reason. Take care, though, as this quality opens you up to being used by others.

TIGER TYPES BY MONTH OF BIRTH

Use the month of your birth to pinpoint your dominant personality type in a single word or phrase.

JANUARY	FEBRUARY	MARCH
Sincere	Efficient	Warmhearted
APRIL	**MAY**	**JUNE**
Independent	Gracious	Lacking vision
JULY	**AUGUST**	**SEPTEMBER**
Energetic	Independent	Well-mannered
OCTOBER	**NOVEMBER**	**DECEMBER**
Lucky	Extroverted	Confident

虎

FENG SHUI ADVICE

Our luck indications change every year, every month, and every day, and the best way to plot this is through the use of a reliable feng shui almanac. The following information is meant as a general guide for the Tiger.

	Lucky	Unlucky
Numbers	1, 3, 4, 13, 34	6, 7, 8, 67, 78
Days	5th, 12th, 27th of the month Success day*: Thursday Vitality day**: Saturday	3rd, 12th, 14th of the month Unlucky day***: Friday
Colors	Green, blue, gray, orange	Red, brown, white, yellow
Directions	Northeast, east, south, northwest	Southwest
Flowers	Daisy, sunflower, lily, cineraria	

* SUCCESS DAY   This day is filled with positive energy and is considered lucky when planning important personal activities or social events.

** VITALITY DAY   This is the day when you are most active and vibrant.

*** UNLUCKY DAY   This day is considered inauspicious and you should avoid it when planning important personal activities or social events.

FENG SHUI FACT

Tigers are believed to possess exorcising power. A painting of a tiger is often hung by the front door of a home in the belief that it will prevent burglary or the entry of evil spirits. Even today, Chinese children wear caps and shoes designed with the tiger image, and sleep on tiger-shaped pillows for protection.

虎

YOUR CHARACTER STRENGTHS

You possess such a strong presence that, when you walk into a room, it seems as if something is about to happen. Strong, courageous, and alert, you have a deep sense of self-reliance, and the intensity of your feelings shows in the way you talk and act. Open and frank, you are willing to speak out your feelings and this earns the trust of others. You rarely regret something you have said.

You are a determined type. Once you make up your mind about something, you do not change it easily. You have difficulty accepting failure and so tend to push yourself hard in pursuit of success. You are one to achieve your life goals through sheer creativity and imagination. You see difficulties as mere opportunities for you to be courageous and have your way. Endowed with confidence and regal bearing, you always impress people with your image of power and authority. You are a source of inspiration to those around you with your straightforwardness and courage. One of your greatest strengths is your sense of fairness and justice, which makes you very adept at straightening out the problems of others.

DOMINANT STRENGTHS	DOMINANT WEAKNESSES
Confident	Argumentative
Tolerant	Temperamental
Loyal	Arrogant
Courageous	Short-tempered
Trustworthy	Hasty
Intelligent	Treacherous
Determined	Outspoken
Fair	Aggressive

虎

PERCEIVED WEAKNESSES

You tend to be easily distracted and are quick to lose your temper. Such impulsive traits can be destructive and might even lead to a downfall, so aim to keep this in check. Learn to wait things out, and you will see favorable results from your efforts. Perseverance is key.

Rare is the occasion on which you do not stand your ground, stick to your principles, or pursue your convictions. An outspoken type, you show no restraint when speaking your mind and expressing your opinions. Though not a weakness in itself, this makes you capable of being brutally blunt with others. You also have a tendency to question authority and convention—it is as if you were born to go against the norm. Take care, as this attitude can cause friction.

Anxious to achieve quick successes and gain instant benefits, you are easily frustrated by failure. If your ideas or thoughts are rejected, you often react in an aggressive way, arguing with others over trivial matters. These are all characteristics of restlessness; if you want to have a satisfying and fulfilling life, you need to temper them.

虎

PROSPECTS FOR YOUR CAREER

You thrive in a competitive environment in which there are plenty of challenges as well as the scope to generate new ideas—you can always be trusted to respond quickly to what is happening around you. However, stability is not a top priority for you. For this reason, you make a great manager, politician, economist, entrepreneur, or advocate for justice issues. Tigers tend to be well connected, which is an asset in networking activities.

EARLY DAYS

Young Tigers can be rather flighty and adventurous—you might find yourself having to change career path frequently. You are also easily frustrated, especially if things do not go as planned. In a nutshell, you may be a high achiever, but you struggle to retain a foothold on success. It can be difficult to overcome setbacks early on, but rest assured that you will gain resilience later in life. Given time, you can develop great leadership skills that will serve you well in your career path. You do not like to take orders from others, so it is advisable to work your way into a position in which you can set your own rules.

A POSITIVE OUTLOOK

You possess great leadership capabilities and knowing this gives you the confidence to work without help from others. Exceptional organizational skills enable you to reach positions of seniority and to gain a good name in your field. You possess an innate desire for control and can be very persuasive, both of which make you a good candidate for the political field. Coupled with a strong sense of justice you may find yourself drawn to fighting against illegal or unfair groups or events.

STRIKE A BALANCE

If you allow yourself to become overconfident in your abilities, you run the risk of disrupting the team effort, which is never useful in a work situation. On the other hand, you need to resist a tendency to waver when it comes to making a decision or to postpone matters that need urgent attention. You also need to learn how to handle negative feedback. Certainly the answer is not to lash out at the person making the criticism. Understand that it is not personal and try to learn from the experience.

PROSPECTS FOR DOMESTIC LIFE

You are skilled at generating income and like nothing more than to share your earnings with your family. Generous to a fault, you want your loved ones to live in comfort and can be impulsive and particular, buying gifts to make them happy.

THE IDEAL HOME

Your home is an extension of your personality: exciting, bright, and fun. You are a yang animal, so will feel constrained living in an environment with yin elements—you find a dark-colored decor and accessories depressing, for example.

Choose wood over metal when it comes to the elements. Thus, wooden furniture is best, but you can also represent wood using plants and flowers inside or outside your home. If there are any metal objects, find less prominent places for them, storing them on shelves or hidden from view. You like to see representations of your zodiac sign; seek out paintings and decorative pieces that feature tigers, or consider owning a pet cat or kitten.

NEAREST AND DEAREST

You may not be the most romantic of signs in the zodiac, but you are a doting parent and have no trouble expressing your aspirations for your children. You want them to excel and you find tremendous joy in watching their talents develop. You like to control family matters, but you are far from authoritarian. You always show willing to listen to your children and to indulge their whims. Intolerant of boredom, you actively participate in your children's upbringing and make the best of companions when it comes to playing physical games and embarking on activities and fun adventures together.

虎

FRIENDSHIP AND LOVE

You are image-conscious, you relish attention, and you take good care of your reputation. A passionate type, you are fearless, full of vigor, and always very clear about what you love or hate. Some find such charm and sincerity hard to resist. However, despite your seemingly tough exterior, you can be both tender and sentimental.

FRIENDS AND LOVERS

You get along best with the Boar—your secret friend—the Horse, Dog, and Tiger. You encounter many love interests, but choose only those who share your penchant for surprises, life aspirations, and great achievements. Therefore, your ideal partner will have a multifaceted personality—someone who can play several roles and, above all, who shares the same liking for adventure in life. You have great faith in love at first sight, and are not interested in wasting your time in pursuit of love. If your show of affection is not reciprocated, you may feel lost. You also value your personal freedom too much to settle down too early in life. Once in a long-term relationship, you maintain your sense of adventure, expecting the partnership to be filled with love and excitement, free from restraint, and always fresh and unpredictable.

FRIENDSHIP WOES

Those born in the signs of the Snake and the Monkey do not make ideal matches for you. Neither are you compatible with those born in the sign of the Ox. Fellow Tigers can sometimes be problematic, too, since they share your strengths and weaknesses and may lack the willingness to accommodate your strong personality.

FRIENDS AND ALLIES

| TIGER | HORSE | DOG |

THE PERFECT MATCH — **BOAR**

THE RABBIT

The Rabbit is the fourth animal in the Chinese zodiac. In Chinese myths and legends, this animal is a symbol of longevity. Affectionate and generous, people born in Rabbit years are considered among the luckiest.

RABBIT YEARS

1927, 1939, 1951, 1963, 1975, 1987, 1999, 2011, 2023, 2035

DATE RANGES FOR THE YEAR OF THE RABBIT

Start Date	End Date	Heavenly Stem	Earthly Branch
February 2, 1927	January 22, 1928	Fire	Wood
February 19, 1939	February 7, 1940	Earth	Wood
February 6, 1951	January 26, 1952	Metal	Wood
January 25, 1963	February 12, 1964	Water	Wood
February 11, 1975	January 30, 1976	Wood	Wood
January 29, 1987	February 16, 1988	Fire	Wood
February 16, 1999	February 4, 2000	Earth	Wood
February 3, 2011	January 22, 2012	Metal	Wood
January 22, 2023	February 9, 2024	Water	Wood
February 8, 2035	January 27, 2036	Wood	Wood

GENERAL CHARACTERISTICS

The Rabbit is a tame and tender animal that moves swiftly, and if you were born in the year of the Rabbit you share these character traits. You are generally modest and have pleasant relationships with those around you. You are not easily provoked to anger and your even temper helps keep you away from conflicts and misunderstandings. Despite that quiet facade, you can be sensitive and will not think twice about moving out of an uneasy situation because you cannot take criticism well.

You have no place for shallow discussions and people admire you for your wit and excellent communication skills. Your skills and sharp memory come in handy in business, particularly in financial matters. You are the type who will not fix anything unless it is broken and would rather go for the old and tested over something that is new but unproven. You have the trappings of a good manager and leader, yet you are also a good follower with high regard for authority and will always gain respect for your loyalty and dedication to your job.

兔

RABBIT TYPES BY YEAR OF BIRTH

You will likely display one of five different personality types, based on your year of birth. The last number of your birth year determines your feng shui element, although you need to pay attention to the cutoff dates so you can determine your animal sign correctly. This is especially important if you were born in either January or February (see The Lunar Calendar, pages 12–13).

1 OR 2	↔	YOUR ELEMENT IS METAL	✛
3 OR 4	↔	YOUR ELEMENT IS WATER	🌊
5 OR 6	↔	YOUR ELEMENT IS WOOD	🌿
7 OR 8	↔	YOUR ELEMENT IS FIRE	🔥
9 OR 0	↔	YOUR ELEMENT IS EARTH	🌑

FIRE RABBIT

1927 ▪ 1987

Witty and outspoken, you of all Rabbit types are most likely to be at the forefront of any activity. You are generous and have a special way of tapping into the strengths of others and handling disagreements. A diplomat of considerable aptitude, you resolve conflicts smoothly and without making enemies in the process—you are genuinely loved and respected for these traits. You set high standards for yourself and expect nothing but the best from those around you. One thing you do need to watch out for is your sudden mood swings, as having a rash reaction to a certain situation could backfire.

EARTH RABBIT

1939 ▪ 1999

Deliberate and logical in your ways, you are a diplomatic type who weighs things up carefully—you are not one to make decisions based on impulse or emotion. This makes you a great team player who can always be trusted to be objective and fair. Despite being an introvert, you have a taste for adventure and do not fear trying new initiatives. You are a trailblazer with sensible ideas. For all your fine taste, you can be quite materialistic and indulgent, and you are not great at managing your finances. Although you are warmhearted, you have a tendency to prioritize your own needs to the detriment of others.

METAL RABBIT

1951 ▪ 2011

You do not give much away, but you have great drive and ambition. You plan quietly and perform impeccably without the need to be in the limelight. Strong beliefs borne out of your intelligence and a keen analysis of situations make you reluctant to compromise. Sheer ambition and a deep sense of responsibility combine with creativity to make you capable of great achievements with the very least of effort. Although you play to your strengths to accomplish things, you do so without stepping on the toes of others.

WATER RABBIT

1963 ▪ 2023

You cannot stand disharmony and so would rather spend time alone than in a big group. This is when you are at your strongest. You tend to follow your heart rather than your head, and are very sensitive to the feelings of others. That same sensitivity sometimes makes you suspicious of a person's motives. At other times you find it difficult to make firm decisions. Try to nurture meaningful relationships with those around you, as having the support of others will enable you to react better to complex situations.

WOOD RABBIT

1975 ▪ 2035

You are the kind of Rabbit that finds it easy to adapt to different situations. You possess all the necessary traits of the ideal team player: stability, reliability, and the acceptance of others. Be wary that the downside to this is a certain fickleness. In attempts to accommodate the different opinions of others, you sometimes find it hard to make your own decisions. A peace-loving type, you are gentle to a fault and avoid challenges lest you offend anyone. You have a generosity that pushes you to excessive spending. Even if this is meant to benefit others, you need to keep tabs on your outgoings if you are going to keep your finances stable.

RABBIT TYPES BY MONTH OF BIRTH

Use the month of your birth to pinpoint your dominant personality type in a single word or phrase.

JANUARY	FEBRUARY	MARCH
Carefree	Graceful	Erratic

APRIL	MAY	JUNE
Conscientious	Uncomplicated	Realistic

JULY	AUGUST	SEPTEMBER
Levelheaded	Determined	Equivocal

OCTOBER	NOVEMBER	DECEMBER
Emotional	Forthright	Self-reliant

兔

FENG SHUI ADVICE

Our luck indications change every year, every month, and every day, and the best way to plot this is through the use of a reliable feng shui almanac. The following information is meant as a general guide for the Rabbit.

	Lucky	Unlucky
Numbers	3, 4, 6, 43, 46	1, 7, 8, 17, 18
Days	11th, 12th, 27th of the month Success day*: Thursday Vitality day**: Saturday	18th, 25th, 26th of the month Unlucky day***: Friday
Colors	Red, green, pink, purple, blue	Dark brown, dark yellow, white
Directions	East, south, northwest	North, west, southwest
Flowers	Arabian jasmine, white jasmine, plantain lily, hosta	

* SUCCESS DAY — This day is filled with positive energy and is considered lucky when planning important personal activities or social events.

** VITALITY DAY — This is the day when you are most active and vibrant.

*** UNLUCKY DAY — This day is considered inauspicious and you should avoid it when planning important personal activities or social events.

FENG SHUI FACT

Chinese tradition has it that you can see a rabbit figure in the moon, and that it is the pet of the Chinese moon goddess Chang'e. As such the rabbit is a symbol of purity and good fortune.

YOUR CHARACTER STRENGTHS

A kind and polite soul, you are adept at handling your relationships. You have many friends and make a good impression on people when meeting them for the first time. You put a premium on your appearance and the way you dress, and this only serves to make you even more popular.

You are known for being organized and are a stickler for order. You are not one to make quick changes or hasty decisions, preferring instead to abide by the maxim, "If it ain't broke, don't fix it." Given the choice, you opt for the tried-and-tested route over a path as yet unproven. Responsible and patient, you always play fair and give credit where it is due. You are an excellent team player.

Of all the animals in the Chinese zodiac, you are perceived to be the luckiest and are likely to enjoy good luck in life. Confident of your talents and skills, you tend to take things lightly, glossing over otherwise significant things. But because of your generally lucky prospects, there are few real challenges for you to face.

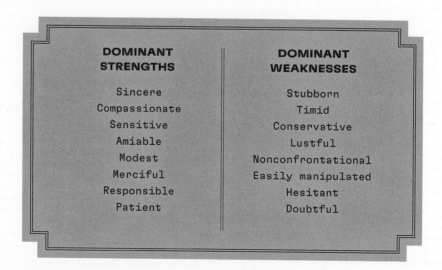

DOMINANT STRENGTHS	DOMINANT WEAKNESSES
Sincere	Stubborn
Compassionate	Timid
Sensitive	Conservative
Amiable	Lustful
Modest	Nonconfrontational
Merciful	Easily manipulated
Responsible	Hesitant
Patient	Doubtful

兔

PERCEIVED WEAKNESSES

Inherently conservative, you may be slow to take action, particularly at the most challenging of times. For this reason, you tend to avoid stressful and risky situations and do not like being forced to make hasty decisions. You have a pessimistic streak that makes you averse to taking risks and prevents you from trusting those around you.

While you are emotionally stable on the whole, you can be quite delicate and cautious at times. As long as you are happy, everything is fine; but if you sense something is wrong, you tend to go out of your way to make it right. This can become problematic and you may find yourself taking a situation too seriously. You may maintain a calm and quiet exterior, but you do not think twice about finding a way out of a tight spot because you cannot handle criticism.

Though your lifestyle is generally peaceful and smooth, you suffer from boredom when things become too predictable. Keep an eye on your finances, as you can be a big spender, with seemingly little concern for the future.

兔

PROSPECTS FOR
YOUR CAREER

Inherently intelligent, you are much admired for your wit and wisdom and for your ability to engage in meaningful conversations. With such excellent communication skills and the respectable manner in which you present yourself, you are the ideal candidate for management positions in the corporate world. That you are also the go-to person for financial matters only supports this.

LEADERSHIP SKILLS   While others may perceive you to be too laid-back, all you really want is to be sure that you are doing things properly. This mindset comes in handy during challenging situations because you are not one to panic; you always have an action plan. As a project leader, you make sure that things go smoothly and according to schedule.

DIVERSE PATHS   Even if you do not find yourself in a position of leadership, you thrive, as you have a high regard for authority and can be counted on for your loyalty and dedication. No matter what path you choose, you prove highly responsible and always apply yourself to the task in hand. Your persistence is such that you do everything you can to stay in your chosen profession. Owing to your aesthetic sensibilities, you may be attracted to creative work. You are good with your hands, for example, making you well placed for jobs that require the handling of manual tools. You are also suitable for jobs that require observation and attention to detail, and thrive in the fields of health care, education, religion, and politics. With your wide social network, you are a fit candidate for PR work.

EMBRACE RISK   Despite your enviable relationship skills, you can be quite reserved. You are not a born risk-taker and prefer to err on the side of caution. Neither do you like competition and you are uncomfortable if pressed to take chances. Take care though, as your propensity for keeping things safe may lead to your missing out on some good opportunities.

PROSPECTS FOR DOMESTIC LIFE

While you are a well-respected model of professionalism at work, at home you are a loving parent who is unconditionally devoted to your children.

PARENTING SKILLS

You possess the energy to fulfill your family duties without much help from others—from monitoring the behavior of your young ones, to helping out with their schoolwork. You are committed to every task that ensures the development of responsible and well-educated children. Right from the start, you try to instill positive values in your offspring. Typically, these young people learn early on that material things are of little consequence. Instead, what is important is creating happy moments with loved ones. You will stop at nothing to ensure that your children enjoy fun-filled occasions and memorable holidays with family and friends.

HOME STYLE

Your home is the essence of Easter, full of pastel colors and child-friendly activities. The Rabbit yang energy should be there in the form of wood furnishings and decor, including paintings of trees and real plants in a lush garden. The metal element is best avoided, as it serves as a reminder of a cage that restricts the movement of the energetic Rabbit. To introduce feelings of warmth and comfort, there should be plenty of fluffy pillows and blankets. Cushions and mattresses must be soft, not firm.

Your home may not be a mansion, but it has most things that are essential to a comfortable lifestyle. Your fine taste shows in the way you furnish the place. You may own some expensive items, perhaps a classy artwork and antiques, but not at the expense of your family's comfort.

兔

FRIENDSHIP AND LOVE

Initially, you exercise caution in both friendly and amorous relationships, but this wariness gradually goes away in time, and you start to open up and become more friendly. You really value your friendships and are popular and admired by the people close to you.

兔

You are most romantically compatible with your secret friend, the Dog, with whom you may fall in love at first glance. The Sheep, the Boar, and the Monkey make good matches, too. Money issues may get in the way of a relationship working with a Snake. Things may also get fraught between you and a Rooster—you are not one to take criticism lightly and Roosters can be a little too outspoken and spontaneous for your liking.

Deeply emotional, you can be somewhat relentless in pursuing a love interest. Coupled with a fragile ego and low self-confidence, you may find yourself worrying too much about a relationship. You can become too attached to a partner, who may find this exhausting or even stifling. Any show of distrust is a red flag—remember this if you want to maintain a happy and stable relationship. You dislike conflict and try to seek compromise whenever possible. This is not always possible, however, so try not to let disappointments get to you.

People in love with you find you mysterious at first. But when they get to know you better, they discover that you are levelheaded and romantic. You can be sensitive, but you can also be considerate. Winning your heart gives you a boost, allowing you to let your tenderness surface and making you an ideal partner for life.

FRIENDS AND ALLIES

RABBIT

SHEEP

BOAR

THE PERFECT MATCH — DOG

THE
DRAGON

The Dragon is the only mythical creature in the Chinese zodiac and is believed to be one of the luckiest among the birth signs. Smart and meticulous, a Dragon sets high standards for itself and tends to be something of a perfectionist in all things.

DRAGON YEARS

1928, 1940, 1952, 1964, 1976, 1988, 2000, 2012, 2024, 2036

DATE RANGES FOR THE YEAR OF THE DRAGON

Start Date	End Date	Heavenly Stem	Earthly Branch
January 23, 1928	February 9, 1929	Earth	Earth
February 8, 1940	January 26, 1941	Metal	Earth
January 27, 1952	February 13, 1953	Water	Earth
February 13, 1964	February 1, 1965	Wood	Earth
January 31, 1976	February 17, 1977	Fire	Earth
February 17, 1988	February 5, 1989	Earth	Earth
February 5, 2000	January 23, 2001	Metal	Earth
January 23, 2012	February 9, 2013	Water	Earth
February 10, 2024	January 28, 2025	Wood	Earth
January 28, 2036	February 14, 2037	Fire	Earth

GENERAL CHARACTERISTICS

If you were born in the year of the Dragon, you have natural charisma and like to do everything on a grand scale. You are also blessed with luck. There is no doubt that you enjoy being the center of attention, but this does not make you uncharitable. You do not hesitate to help a friend in need, and when everyone else has given up, you step forward to resolve a problem with authority and dignity.

Your positivity shines through even the most difficult of situations. Your openness somehow balances your offensive views and others still give you credit for your exciting takes on issues regardless of how controversial they are. You are quick to trust others—something that should not be abused, because it is difficult for you to forgive once that trust is betrayed.

You are gifted with power, which you usually handle well, but you can be egoistical, ambitious, and snobbish. At times you will stop at nothing to get what you want. It is wise to keep a check on this, as you risk becoming aggressive, determined, and dominant to your own detriment.

✳ DRAGON TYPES BY YEAR OF BIRTH

You will likely display one of five different personality types, based on your year of birth. The last number of your birth year determines your feng shui element, although you need to pay attention to the cutoff dates so you can determine your animal sign correctly. This is especially important if you were born in either January or February (see The Lunar Calendar, pages 12–13).

0 OR 1	↔	YOUR ELEMENT IS METAL	✛
2 OR 3	↔	YOUR ELEMENT IS WATER	🌊
4 OR 5	↔	YOUR ELEMENT IS WOOD	🌿
6 OR 7	↔	YOUR ELEMENT IS FIRE	🔥
8 OR 9	↔	YOUR ELEMENT IS EARTH	✿

EARTH DRAGON

1928 ▪ 1988

The friendliest Dragon type, you are also the most stable and levelheaded. However, while you are likable, you come across as impersonal because you tend to favor practical and realistic things over more fun or unconventional ones. This common-sense approach makes you a well-rounded person with solid moral convictions. You spend a good deal of time on self-introspection and have the motivation to improve yourself—it will not take long to develop your innate talents through patience and hard work. You generate wealth, owing to your business expertise and creativity, and use this for the good of others.

METAL DRAGON

1940 ▪ 2000

Endowed with great power and strength, you are a natural leader. While you are happy to work independently, you use your winning personality to build a supportive team around you. You are truly compelling, and every pronouncement manifests as an invitation to succeed. You never back down from a challenge and failure simply is not an option. You have little tolerance for laziness and complacency. You may not realize it, but you can be critical while expressing your views.

WATER DRAGON

1952 ▪ 2012

Unlike the other Dragon types, you are calm and collected. Beneath your relaxed appearance is a mind capable of great clarity and balance—the kind of mind that makes you an effective negotiator. You take the time to think things through before making your moves. You are hardworking, have a good sense of humor, and show restraint to hold off your thoughts when necessary. Free of any sense of entitlement, you do not consider it a failure when a door closes in your face; rather, you accept it as part of the learning process that is life.

WOOD DRAGON

1964 ▪ 2024

Naturally curious about the things around you, you are not afraid of exploring the unfamiliar. Not easily daunted by what other people say, you take it upon yourself to blaze a trail where there is none and your fearlessness attracts good fortune. Gifted with a creative character, people adore you for your generosity and innovative ideas. Unlike other Dragon types, you are nonconfrontational; you rarely step on the toes of others and always choose harmony over discord.

FIRE DRAGON

1976 ▪ 2036

The most competitive of all Dragons, you are brimming with ambition and set high standards in all aspects of your life. You have refined taste in music and the arts and to some you may seem aloof. Your desirable communication skills are useful for advancing your career and earn you the respect and admiration of others. You make a great leader owing to your strong beliefs, but you need to control your temper and authoritarian approach. You have a tendency to let your feelings rule your actions, which could harm your prospects. You are also prone to favoring your own judgment with little regard for the feelings of others.

DRAGON TYPES BY MONTH OF BIRTH

Use the month of your birth to pinpoint your dominant personality type in a single word or phrase.

JANUARY	FEBRUARY	MARCH
Courteous	Logical	Overbearing
APRIL	**MAY**	**JUNE**
Generous	Affectionate	Principled
JULY	**AUGUST**	**SEPTEMBER**
Hardworking	Vigilant	Prudent
OCTOBER	**NOVEMBER**	**DECEMBER**
Tenacious	Perceptive	Purposeful

FENG SHUI ADVICE

Our luck indications change every year, every month, and every day, and the best way to plot this is through the use of a reliable feng shui almanac. The following information is meant as a general guide for the Dragon.

	Lucky	Unlucky
Numbers	1, 6, 7, 16, 17	3, 8, 38, 83
Days	3rd, 6th, 12th of the month Success day*: Sunday Vitality day**: Wednesday	8th, 9th, 11th of the month Unlucky day***: Thursday
Colors	Beige, gold, silver, gray, white	Black, brown
Directions	Southeast, east, west, southwest	Northwest
Flowers	Bleeding heart vine, glory bower, dragon flower	

* SUCCESS DAY	This day is filled with positive energy and is considered lucky when planning important personal activities or social events.
** VITALITY DAY	This is the day when you are most active and vibrant.
*** UNLUCKY DAY	This day is considered inauspicious and you should avoid it when planning important personal activities or social events.

FUN FACT

The Dragon has become the subject of many popular Chinese sayings and idioms. For example, wishing that a parent's child "becomes a dragon" means you want that child to be successful. The expression "a dragon among men" refers to an exceptionally talented person.

YOUR CHARACTER STRENGTHS

A natural leader, you are careful about the people you choose to surround yourself with. Those in your closest circle are there owing to the loyalty and kindness they are willing to give you. You have strong leadership qualities and people have no issues following you because they trust your knowledge and capabilities implicitly.

Owing to your friendly nature, you are well liked and invariably find yourself in the limelight, where your lively presence never fails to get attention. And you thrive on attention. Even in the most difficult of situations, your positivity shines through, earning you the respect of those around you.

You have great confidence in your views and do not hesitate to give your opinion on things, regardless of what others might think. You are firm and sure about what you want and work tirelessly in pursuit of your dreams. Neither your luck nor your energy seem to have any bounds, and you believe in seizing the moment.

PERCEIVED WEAKNESSES

A perfectionist, you often criticize others if they do not meet your high standards. Your lack of tact lands you in trouble, but you are able to counter this at times with your openness. Though you are quick to trust others, you find it a real challenge to forgive someone who crosses or betrays you. Impatient and intolerant of delays, you tend to act impulsively. Once you have made a decision to act, you do so immediately rather than just watch things go by.

That aura of leadership that some people see in you can be perceived as being too authoritative or arrogant. An inability to be totally transparent with your emotions leaves people with the impression that you are being icy or aloof. Your sense of power can manifest as aggressiveness, which can cloud your judgment. Worse still, it can cost you friendships. Many of these weaknesses stem from your self-confidence, which can be overbearing. Look for ways to temper this overconfidence, and you will make life less difficult for yourself.

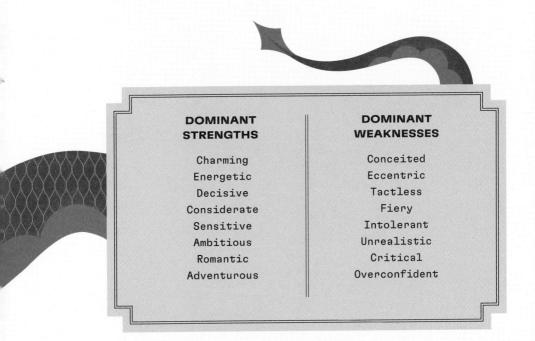

DOMINANT STRENGTHS	DOMINANT WEAKNESSES
Charming	Conceited
Energetic	Eccentric
Decisive	Tactless
Considerate	Fiery
Sensitive	Intolerant
Ambitious	Unrealistic
Romantic	Critical
Adventurous	Overconfident

PROSPECTS FOR YOUR CAREER

You are the embodiment of firm determination and solid ambition. A quick thinker, you excel in fields that others find mentally draining. Better still, you think openly, and make a good leader if you are given free rein to develop your ideas. Careers that suit you are those in politics, media/public relations, and entertainment where your outgoing personality is given room to shine.

TEAM LEADER

Adventurous, ambitious, and highly driven, once you have set your goals, you try your best to achieve success. Your innate passion shows in how you project yourself—with eloquence and authority. You are very charming and find it easy to win the support of others. Your ideal setup is at the head of a team. You have the vision, are great at planning and coming up with ideas, but you need the help of others to make them happen. While self-confidence has a key role to play here, it can hinder your personal development. Remember: you need to tone it down a little if you want to create lasting relationships.

NEW HORIZONS

Your career efforts bear fruit by the time you reach 40, but things may take a downturn as you grow older. You do not have problems making money—which, after all, is not the most important thing in your life—but you may face challenges that take persistence to overcome. Creating new opportunities is the key to your having a rich and stable midlife. Aside from your boundless energy, you have another gift: luck. Take advantage of this good luck and your brilliant leadership skills to build a successful career and make a difference in whatever field or profession you choose.

龙

PROSPECTS FOR
DOMESTIC LIFE

A house with a Dragon influence has little lacking. In the same way that you know how to build an empire, you are ready and willing to share your wealth and treasures with family members. You know your personal worth and are generous with kind words and material provisions.

A WELCOMING ENVIRONMENT

All Dragons need to tell people—family members included—about their ideas, and you are no exception. You love a good gathering, with friends and family members as your audience. Your home needs to have a large, welcoming space in which to accommodate guests, who should not feel cramped or restricted in their movements. You love to exhibit your wealth and good fortune, and your home is your way of showing others that you are a good provider.

Metal is a positive element for you and, true enough, you like the colors gold and silver and things that shine. You also feel comfortable with the colors red and yellow, but not with green and blue. You fill your home with lights—all sorts of lamps and decorative candles to set a happy mood.

A DOMINEERING TYPE

Strong-willed, you are not afraid to face challenges outside or inside of your home, and this can make you quite demanding of those who live under your roof. As a parent, you are determined to raise independent children, and want them to grow up to be just like you. Though you do this out of good intentions and deep love, you must take care not to be too domineering. Resist the urge to pressurize your offspring if you consider them to lack the drive to succeed. Allow them to develop their talents and make achievements in their own time. Above all, try to keep your temper in check—you are easily provoked and are prone to outbursts that you later come to regret.

FRIENDSHIP AND LOVE

Naturally, your innate desire for perfection extends to your relationships with others. In your search for the ideal partner, you initially feel unsure and hesitant in making a permanent commitment. But once you take the initiative, you want a relationship to last.

COMPATIBILITY

An outgoing type, you are highly compatible with your secret friend, the Rooster. You will find good friends and allies in the Monkey, the Rat, and fellow Dragons. You also do well with the Tiger, the Snake, the Rabbit, and the Horse. However, you may not agree with the Dog or the Ox, who tend to be a little on the quiet side for you. Moreover, your conflicting styles threaten to overwhelm a relationship. You also struggle to work with the Tiger, because you both have solid and aggressive personalities, which inevitably clash.

SLOW STARTER

Having such an independent streak leads you to shun romantic relationships, even if you have many admirers who fall for your charm and good looks. You also tend to be quite passive and are not one to go into active pursuit of your love interest—your preference is to let a relationship develop naturally. Once you are committed however—which tends to happen late in life—you prove to be an honest and generous partner and enjoy a smooth and harmonious life.

FRIENDS AND ALLIES	RAT	DRAGON	MONKEY

THE PERFECT MATCH — ROOSTER

WHEEL

愛

THE DOG · THE BOAR · THE RAT · THE OX · THE TIGER · THE RABBIT · THE DRAGON · THE SNAKE · THE HORSE · THE SHEEP · THE MONKEY · THE ROOSTER

OF
LOVE

COMPATIBILITY KEY

♥ Rat, Dragon, Monkey

♥ Ox, Snake, Rooster

♥ Tiger, Horse, Dog

♥ Rabbit, Sheep, Boar

U se the wheel of love to find the most compatible animals for lasting relationships. Just follow the "triangular" formula to find the best matches for you.

PERFECT PAIRINGS

Besides the friends and allies of triangular formula, each animal also has a "secret friend." Secret friends often make the best lovers.

RAT	↔	OX
BOAR	↔	TIGER
DOG	↔	RABBIT
SHEEP	↔	HORSE
MONKEY	↔	SNAKE
ROOSTER	↔	DRAGON

BAD MATCHES

To find your least compatible partner, simply see which sign sits directly opposite yours on the wheel. In Chinese astrology, opposites do not attract!

RAT	↔	HORSE
OX	↔	SHEEP
TIGER	↔	MONKEY
RABBIT	↔	ROOSTER
DRAGON	↔	DOG
SNAKE	↔	BOAR

THE
SNAKE

The Snake is the sixth animal in the order of the Chinese zodiac. Inherently innovative, it is a fitting symbol of knowledge. Charming and intuitive, the Snake is considered the wisest and most enigmatic of all animal signs.

SNAKE YEARS

1929, 1941, 1953, 1965, 1977, 1989, 2001, 2013, 2025, 2037

DATE RANGES FOR THE YEAR OF THE SNAKE

Start Date	End Date	Heavenly Stem	Earthly Branch
February 10, 1929	January 29, 1930	Earth	Fire
January 27, 1941	February 14, 1942	Metal	Fire
February 14, 1953	February 2, 1954	Water	Fire
February 2, 1965	January 20, 1966	Wood	Fire
February 18, 1977	February 6, 1978	Fire	Fire
February 6, 1989	January 26, 1990	Earth	Fire
February 24, 2001	February 11, 2002	Metal	Fire
February 10, 2013	January 30, 2014	Water	Fire
January 29, 2025	February 16, 2026	Wood	Fire
February 15, 2037	February 3, 2038	Fire	Fire

GENERAL
CHARACTERISTICS

You may have little to say, but you possess great wisdom. You are determined in everything you do and hate to fail. Because of this—and the fact that you do not always trust the judgment of others—you prefer to rely on yourself and even tend to overdo things. Calm on the surface, you are an intense and passionate type. You have tremendous sympathy for others and often try to help those less fortunate than yourself. This does not stop you from being a little vain, however, and you can be both selfish and stingy.

Financially fortunate, you never have to worry about money. You are likely to be good-looking and might experience relationship problems because you are fickle. You value your privacy and tend to keep secrets. This does not qualify you as an ideal team player and makes you seem aloof at times; however, this weakness is offset by your high energy levels and passion for getting things done. You will not settle for being second-rate, and with your talents, you can easily keep up with the best there is.

✳ SNAKE TYPES BY YEAR OF BIRTH

You will likely display one of five different personality types, based on your year of birth. The last number of your birth year determines your feng shui element, although you need to pay attention to the cutoff dates so you can determine your animal sign correctly. This is especially important if you were born in either January or February (see The Lunar Calendar, pages 12–13).

1 OR 2	↔	YOUR ELEMENT IS METAL	✛
3 OR 4	↔	YOUR ELEMENT IS WATER	〰
5 OR 6	↔	YOUR ELEMENT IS WOOD	♨
7 OR 8	↔	YOUR ELEMENT IS FIRE	🔥
9 OR 0	↔	YOUR ELEMENT IS EARTH	⬢

EARTH SNAKE

1929 ▪ 1989

You may not be as intense as the other Snake types, but you are more grounded and levelheaded, approaching tasks with disciplined pace and perseverance. Still, you have the same sincerity and effortless leadership qualities as your Snake siblings. Practical and reliable, you are capable of managing diverse situations. You are also good with your finances, ensuring stability and steady progress. You exude warmth and are sensitive to the feelings of others—traits that bring you loyal friends and supporters.

METAL SNAKE

1941 ▪ 2001

Although typically a quiet soul, you do not lack self-confidence.
Your incredible focus and intelligent ways make you one of the most
driven animal signs. Highly competitive, you will spare no effort to be
on top, and because of this you are not one to be crossed. You select
friends carefully, usually drawing on a small social circle of like-
minded people who also enjoy the arts, music, and the finer things
in life. You set high store on building wealth in order to acquire
material luxuries.

WATER SNAKE

1953 ▪ 2013

Versatile and capable of handling different things simultaneously,
you have varied interests and can excel in all of them. This flexibility,
coupled with your eye for projects that bring good profits, makes
you very effective in handling matters related to money. You are
an asset to any group with your strength in getting the best out
of people to meet business goals. While it is difficult to make you
lose focus, you have a good sense of what is practical and are
always open to other ideas.

WOOD SNAKE

1965 ▪ 2025

Hugely approachable, very open, and easy to communicate with, you are the most charismatic of all Snake types. Your great perseverance bolsters relationships, making you an emotionally stable and loyal friend—it is no wonder you are able to attract lasting friends and good fortune. Still, you are not easily satisfied, but rather seek new knowledge and use it to improve life for yourself and the people you love. You value recognition and so are meticulous with your physical appearance and relentless in pursuing the goals you have set for yourself.

FIRE SNAKE

1977 ▪ 2037

A self-assured type, you have an intensity that allows you to excel in whatever you choose to do, and magnetic leader-like traits that inspire others. You are intuitive and possess an emotional stability that serves you well in such areas as politics and public relations. Your innate charm and dynamism could help you succeed in a career that puts you in the limelight—perhaps as a performer. You set big goals and with your high energy levels and determination, you give everything you have to achieve them. Expect to reap wealth and recognition as due rewards.

SNAKE TYPES BY MONTH OF BIRTH

Use the month of your birth to pinpoint your dominant personality type in a single word or phrase.

JANUARY	FEBRUARY	MARCH
Forward-looking	Indecisive	Skeptical
APRIL	**MAY**	**JUNE**
Presumptuous	Egoistical	Lively
JULY	**AUGUST**	**SEPTEMBER**
Flexible	Inquisitive	Daring
OCTOBER	**NOVEMBER**	**DECEMBER**
Frivolous	Progressive	Honest

FENG SHUI ADVICE

Our luck indications change every year, every month, and every day, and the best way to plot this is through the use of a reliable feng shui almanac. The following information is meant as a general guide for the Snake.

	Lucky	Unlucky
Numbers	2, 8, 9, 28, 29	1, 6, 7, 16, 17
Days	6th, 12th, 13th of the month Success day*: Tuesday Vitality day**: Friday	6th, 8th, 9th of the month Unlucky day***: Wednesday
Colors	Red, pink, purple, green	Black, blue, white
Directions	East, west, southwest	Northeast, northwest
Flowers	*Brassavola* orchid, *Catasetum* orchid, cactus	

* SUCCESS DAY   This day is filled with positive energy and is considered lucky when planning important personal activities or social events.

** VITALITY DAY   This is the day when you are most active and vibrant.

*** UNLUCKY DAY   This day is considered inauspicious and you should avoid it when planning important personal activities or social events.

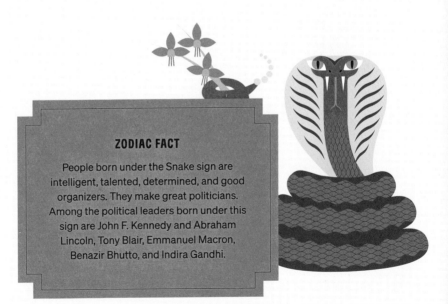

ZODIAC FACT

People born under the Snake sign are intelligent, talented, determined, and good organizers. They make great politicians. Among the political leaders born under this sign are John F. Kennedy and Abraham Lincoln, Tony Blair, Emmanuel Macron, Benazir Bhutto, and Indira Gandhi.

YOUR CHARACTER STRENGTHS

A great communicator, you nevertheless choose to say very little, and others may take you for an introvert. In truth, however, you are extremely intuitive and a great thinker. You are also strong-willed and have no trouble standing your ground. You can be quite materialistic and do not settle easily for second best. For this reason, you like to stay ahead of the curve.

Intent on achieving the goals you set, you work hard to conceive a system to accomplish them. Once you settle on your objectives, you work relentlessly until you see the end in sight. You know your strengths and do not accept failure easily. It is usually effortless for you to spring back from your mistakes. The Snake is possibly the most mysterious animal sign in the Chinese zodiac. Some say that the ability of the snake to shed its skin also reflects the strong regenerative capacity of Snake people to recover quickly from a difficult stage in life.

PERCEIVED WEAKNESSES

If you were born in the year of the Snake, you may tend toward being highly secretive, lacking in generosity, and sometimes suspicious of others. You may not have many real friends because of this, but you are actually quite comfortable with only a few people around you. Ironically, you can be nosy about the personal affairs of others and like to spread rumors. You can be envious of people who appear to be more capable than you and tend to keep such people out of your circle rather than learn from them.

You do not always make the best team player and can sometimes appear aloof. Neither do you always appear to have clear motivations for your actions. Although you are ambitious, you sometimes lack the persistence to see your goals through and can even be quite lazy. Or perhaps you tire yourself out quickly owing to your high energy levels and passion for getting things done. It is at times like this that you tend to turn to self-reflection to restore your depleted energy. Unless you do something to counter this, you may be vulnerable to the unwanted effects of stress. Try to pace yourself.

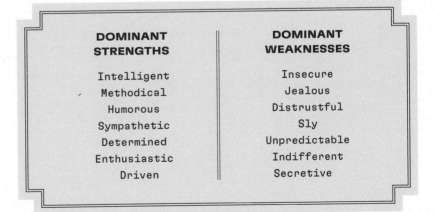

DOMINANT STRENGTHS	DOMINANT WEAKNESSES
Intelligent	Insecure
Methodical	Jealous
Humorous	Distrustful
Sympathetic	Sly
Determined	Unpredictable
Enthusiastic	Indifferent
Driven	Secretive

PROSPECTS FOR YOUR CAREER

If you were born under the sign of the Snake, you are tenacious and sensible. You easily adapt to whatever environment you find yourself in and respond quickly to different situations. You are fully aware of your capabilities, which, coupled with your strong intuition, enable you to seize good opportunities when they present themselves.

LIKELY CAREERS

Snakes keep very high standards in life and are often proficient in various fields. You may see your skills best used in research, writing, and in any work environment where you can apply your creative ideas. You will also do well in social work, public services, human resources, teaching, and politics. You have such an unquenchable taste for learning that science and mathematics may be your calling. You also have a grace and feel for rhythm that will help you excel as a dancer and performer.

SLOW BUT STEADY

Relatively slow in making decisions, you tend to take your time and may bloom late in your chosen career. It is also not uncommon for you to hop from one job to another until you find the security you seek. But you are not afraid of a challenge and are not the type to give up easily. Given your strong sense of responsibility, you handle difficulties with efficiency. You have a sharp memory and are good at remembering names and faces. At work, you are not known to flaunt your achievements, preferring rather to work slowly but surely following set plans. Because you are smart, your chances of getting promoted are high, your leadership qualities allowing you to move far up the career ladder.

PROSPECTS FOR DOMESTIC LIFE

Though you strive hard to earn your money, you enjoy showering your loved ones with luxurious gifts and taking them out to dine or travel. There are no limits to the love you show those who matter to you. Consequently, you feel frustrated when people betray that affection or if you do not get the respect and obedience you expect.

HOME LIFE

You tend to be rather sluggish around the home, preferring to lead a quite life with a well-planned routine. As a parent, you may unwittingly try to control your children's affairs. You view this as your supreme duty to play the role of guardian angel, thinking that your influence will ultimately benefit the future of your offspring. You indulge in meaningful and intellectual conversations, but would rather be an observer than a participant in physical activities—for playmates, your children will need to look elsewhere.

HOME STYLE

You are a complicated being, represented by the fire element and yin energy. This means that the energy in your home should have both yin and yang elements. Ideally, there should be lots of earth, water, and perhaps metal elements. Earth can take the form of clay or brick ornaments and ceramic figurines. The fire element can be expressed by the color red and triangular-shaped objects (because a triangle points upward like a flame). Your living room may benefit from displaying a range of shapes because a snake itself can adopt different forms: it can coil into a circle, it can stretch out long, and it can squeeze through triangular and square gaps. Try to include a mix of practical and outlandish furnishings. One thing you must have is a place for hiding precious collections and a secret room where you can find a little solitude—somewhere that is not too busy or cluttered.

蛇

FRIENDSHIP AND LOVE

When it comes to personal relationships, you are often difficult to fathom. Your idea of love is different from that of most people and it takes a little patience to find out what you really want from a relationship.

BEST AND WORST RELATIONSHIPS

You will develop the most meaningful relationships with people born in the year of the Monkey. Like you, Monkeys are clever and ambitious and you can learn a lot from each other. Fellow Snakes, Roosters, and Dragons make good friends and allies. Think twice about choosing Tigers who, like you, are just too secretive. You will also fail to see eye-to-eye with the Rabbit, the Snake, and the Boar. All of these bring such different characteristics into the mix and it is difficult to make a relationship last.

THE SNAKE IN LOVE

Having found true love, you can seem unenthusiastic or indifferent at times, and this may drive people away. Much of the problem lies in the fact that you are not open about your true feelings. However, once you warm up to a new acquaintance, you are both chatty and passionate. You want to make sure that you have common interests and tend to have high standards for romantic partners. Once in love, you reveal your true fiery soul. Your heart overrules your mind and this surprising contrast wins favor from the object of your attention.

LONG-TERM RELATIONSHIPS

You may regard a long-term relationship and marriage as rather humdrum—merely the final step after the more exciting game of pursuit and courtship, which you are very good at. This can be frustrating to a partner. Once committed, you expect utmost loyalty from your partner—something that you, yourself, find difficult to offer.

FRIENDS AND ALLIES	OX	SNAKE	ROOSTER

THE PERFECT MATCH — **MONKEY**

THE
HORSE

E nergetic and perceptive, the Horse is the seventh animal in the order of the Chinese zodiac. Owing to its high-spirited and active nature, it has come to symbolize freedom, power, and beauty in Chinese culture.

HORSE YEARS

1930, 1942, 1954, 1966, 1978, 1990, 2002, 2014, 2026, 2038

DATE RANGES FOR THE YEAR OF THE HORSE

Start Date	End Date	Heavenly Stem	Earthly Branch
January 30, 1930	February 16, 1931	Metal	Fire
February 15, 1942	February 4, 1943	Water	Fire
February 3, 1954	January 23, 1955	Wood	Fire
January 21, 1966	February 8, 1967	Fire	Fire
February 7, 1978	January 27, 1979	Earth	Fire
January 27, 1990	February 14, 1991	Metal	Fire
February 12, 2002	January 31, 2003	Water	Fire
January 31, 2014	February 18, 2015	Wood	Fire
February 17, 2026	February 5, 2027	Fire	Fire
February 4, 2038	January 23, 2039	Earth	Fire

GENERAL
CHARACTERISTICS

Born to run, you are an active, physical being,
a hard worker, and productive in all that you
do. You are talented and good with your hands.
You have an independent streak that borders on
rebelliousness. Cunning and full of street-smarts,
you rarely listen to advice. You hate to be pressured
or told what to do. Simply bursting with energy, you
shine at social events and love to be in the spotlight.
You are cheerful, wise with money, and perceptive,
although sometimes you talk too much.

Beneath your beguiling character, you may not
be adept at keeping your feelings hidden and will
quickly show your anger when incited. You have
no tolerance for dullness and boredom, and for you
to feel fulfilled especially in your job, there has to be
something new and vital in the tasks at hand. Your
boundless energy seeks a certain type of excitement
to keep you going. You need to have a handle on
this, though. Because of your fluctuating interests,
you might lose your focus and leave a few
undertakings uncompleted.

HORSE TYPES BY YEAR OF BIRTH

You will likely display one of five different personality types, based on your year of birth. The last number of your birth year determines your feng shui element, although you need to pay attention to the cutoff dates so you can determine your animal sign correctly. This is especially important if you were born in either January or February (see The Lunar Calendar, pages 12–13).

0 OR 1	↔	YOUR ELEMENT IS METAL	✛
2 OR 3	↔	YOUR ELEMENT IS WATER	🐦
4 OR 5	↔	YOUR ELEMENT IS WOOD	🌿
6 OR 7	↔	YOUR ELEMENT IS FIRE	✋
8 OR 9	↔	YOUR ELEMENT IS EARTH	✿

METAL HORSE

1930 ▪ 1990

Extremely driven and focused, you are probably the most independent of all Horse types. Your energy levels are so high that others find it difficult to keep pace with you. You are highly capable and seldom need help completing tasks. You do not take kindly to anyone breathing down your neck and can become stubborn or bored if you are not able to do things your way. Despite this, you have many friends because you have such a warm and friendly character. One thing to be mindful of is that you find it hard to make commitments that threaten to hamper your independence.

WATER HORSE

1942 ▪ 2002

A cheerful person, you are conversant in many topics and are
therefore liked by many. You have diverse talents and excel in many
areas. Your love for the great outdoors takes you to interesting
places. Like your water element, you are comfortable in almost
any situation and with people from all walks of life. Your high level
of adaptability allows you to make necessary changes even
in difficult times, making you an ideal fit in careers that
require good interpersonal relations.

WOOD HORSE

1954 ▪ 2014

You have a good head on your shoulders, brimming with ideas that
are both practical and innovative. You are not averse to casting off
old beliefs in favor of new ways for as long as they work, and while
you value your independence, you are also open to meeting your
peers halfway. You always stay grounded and are able to juggle
several activities that require efficiency and organizational skills.
Unlike other Horse types, you are more disciplined and can be
trusted to see projects through to completion. Strong social skills
see you cultivating a large circle of friends and amiable relationships.

FIRE HORSE

1966 ▪ 2026

You are probably the wildest among all Horse types. Highly intelligent and courageous, you are a risk-taker, you are very competitive, and you do not back down easily. You set extraordinarily high standards for yourself, which is great ... until you get bored or offended by people who do not share your views. This can become problematic because your explosive nature surfaces the moment you lose focus or become distracted.

EARTH HORSE

1978 ▪ 2038

The most likable of all Horse types, you exercise more caution in your actions and words than other Horse types do. You weigh things up carefully before making a decision, which can make you indecisive at times. You have a set of principles that you adhere to closely, but you are more open to the ideas of others. You are a deep thinker, with a soft side that reveals you to be both generous and sensitive. You always bring a positive energy to the situations in which you find yourself. With a good eye for promising investments, you can be trusted to save faltering ventures and work out better returns for some humdrum initiatives.

HORSE TYPES BY MONTH OF BIRTH

Use the month of your birth to pinpoint your dominant personality type in a single word or phrase.

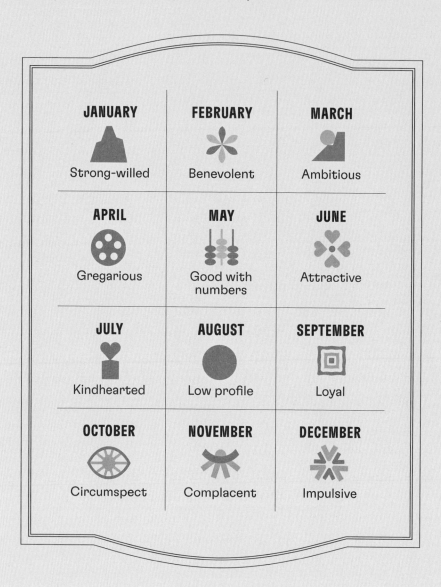

JANUARY	FEBRUARY	MARCH
Strong-willed	Benevolent	Ambitious

APRIL	MAY	JUNE
Gregarious	Good with numbers	Attractive

JULY	AUGUST	SEPTEMBER
Kindhearted	Low profile	Loyal

OCTOBER	NOVEMBER	DECEMBER
Circumspect	Complacent	Impulsive

FENG SHUI ADVICE

Our luck indications change every year, every month, and every day, and the best way to plot this is through the use of a reliable feng shui almanac. The following information is meant as a general guide for the Horse.

	Lucky	Unlucky
Numbers	2, 3, 7, 23, 27	1, 5, 6, 15, 16
Days	6th, 12th, 17th of the month Success day*: Tuesday Vitality day**: Friday	5th, 20th, 27th of the month Unlucky day***: Wednesday
Colors	Yellow, red, green	Blue, gray, black
Directions	South, east, west	North, northwest
Flowers	Plantain lily, hosta "francee" ornamental	

* SUCCESS DAY — This day is filled with positive energy and is considered lucky when planning important personal activities or social events.

** VITALITY DAY — This is the day when you are most active and vibrant.

*** UNLUCKY DAY — This day is considered inauspicious and you should avoid it when planning important personal activities or social events.

ZODIAC FACT

In the legendary race to decide the Chinese zodiac order, the Horse surprisingly fared poorly, despite its ability to gallop. But during the race, the Snake secretly coiled itself around the Horse's hoof. At the finish line, the Snake quickly uncoiled itself and slid forward to claim the sixth place. The startled Horse had to take a step back in surprise and landed in the seventh slot.

YOUR CHARACTER STRENGTHS

A social creature, you prefer to interact with fellow Horses. Careful and deliberate in your ways, you make great efforts to pay attention to others. You are mild-mannered and can be very generous to your friends.

Well connected, you are appreciated by many for your brilliant mind, your trustworthiness, and your vivacious personality. You are courageous and may even be considered free-spirited, yet you are firmly grounded. Exceptionally coordinated, you do not pull out of a challenge. Horses born with these qualities go on to accomplish much in this world.

You are not one to tolerate dullness. In order to feel fulfilled, your work needs to offer constant excitement. Even if you are tired, you still find a way to get fired up and engaged in the task at hand. A great strength of yours is that you understand the significance of time and cash. You avoid unnecessary spending and rarely go over budget. There are very few Horses who find themselves in financial difficulties, even if wealth is not a prime goal in life.

DOMINANT STRENGTHS

Self-sufficient	Generous
Warmhearted	Reliable
Financial whiz	Energetic
Upright	
Easygoing	

PERCEIVED WEAKNESSES

You might find others on their guard when in your company. This is likely because your interests tend to fluctuate and you sometimes shy away from important undertakings. You might enter into a task or activity positively but turn your back on it and give up if things do not seem to be going your way. You easily lose focus, leaving tasks uncompleted, and others perceive you as having a low sense of duty.

There is nothing you will do in exchange for your freedom. You are not one to feel obligated to anybody—you like to work to your own rhythm and tend to listen only to your internal voice. This gives others the impression that you are not very flexible.

You can be a little oversensitive. You have a keen sense of the way others treat you and easily take offence. Careless words anger you. Because you are not very good at managing your feelings, you are quick to show your outrage when provoked. Despite being difficult and egoistic at times, you actually intrigue others with your generosity and impeccable humor. Learn to overcome your restlessness, and these traits will bring you the rewards you strive toward.

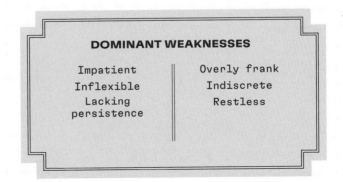

DOMINANT WEAKNESSES

Impatient	Overly frank
Inflexible	Indiscrete
Lacking persistence	Restless

PROSPECTS FOR YOUR CAREER

Career-wise, you are always at your best if playing to your strengths in performing challenging tasks that require constant change and innovation. You prefer not to have a fixed nine-to-five schedule and like to be giving the orders rather than taking them.

SUITABLE ROLES

If you are an efficient type, you work well in the field of journalism, which keeps you on your toes, or in stockbroking, which requires making decisions based on fast-changing developments. Your adaptability, eloquence, and quick wit come to the fore in media hosting, sales, or politics. Your enduring energy and stamina serve you well as an exceptional athlete. You are restless and love to travel, which boosts your potential in pursuing jobs related to tourism.

THE RIGHT BALANCE

With your character strengths, you can be successful in whatever career you choose. However, you must acknowledge your weaknesses, otherwise you may encounter difficulties along the way. You need to be more open to advice and criticism and learn to trust others. You may well be career-oriented and innovative, but you lack patience, can be impulsive, and are prone to giving up. Try to be more persevering and patient rather than abandoning a project halfway.

You may experience setbacks while developing your career. No matter what comes, however, you reap great achievements for which you can expect respect and admiration from others. Because you are such a social individual, you have many friends who can help you hurdle challenges along the way. Build on your experiences, and you will be able to maintain your status at work and enjoy the odd promotion to boot.

PROSPECTS FOR DOMESTIC LIFE

You are so easy to love that you will likely have several relationships before you finally settle down. Once you make this big move, you are very faithful to your partner. With total commitment to family life, you think of every opportunity to provide for the needs and comfort of those around you, and even get them to share and enjoy your great thirst for fun and adventure.

HAPPY HOME

You are a welcoming host and arrange many happy occasions at home. As a parent, you thrive on bonding with all members of your family. You pamper your children and treasure even their smallest achievements. You share your admirable manual skills with your offspring, who, just like you, develop skills that will serve them well later in life. It is not unusual for your children to know their way in the kitchen or to fix broken things.

RECREATIONAL VIBE

The Horse home reflects its owner's vibrant character. Yours is colorful, inspired by sunshine, and fun. It is also full of facilities for active recreation. Allow the yang elements of wood, fire, and earth to dominate, using the colors red and orange, bright lights, and technological gadgets to represent them.

Each area of your home should have distinct features to reflect your interests. Your active lifestyle may require a recreation and exercise room for family members to work out in. There should also be a room spacious enough to include various fitness or sing-along equipment and to allow dancing both for fun and wellness.

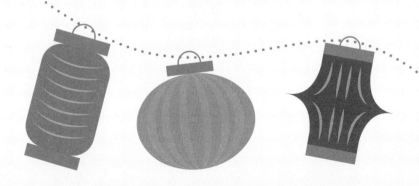

FRIENDSHIP AND LOVE

If you were born under the sign of the Horse, you probably know already that you are lucky in love. Charming and cheerful, you are a good dresser, all of which contributes to your popularity with others. Honest and nonconfrontational, if you do not see a future in a relationship, you simply walk away and find a more promising one.

COMPATIBILITY

Anyone looking to have a relationship with you must also love challenge and adventure. The ideal romantic partners for the Horse are the Tiger, the Dog, and the Sheep. The last is your secret friend and so makes the best match. Tigers make excellent partners because they share the same interests, including outdoor activities, nature trips, and parties. Horses are also compatible, as are Snakes, Rabbits, Dragons, and Boars. However, you do not work well with the down-to-earth Ox or the overcautious Rat. A partnership with the wily Monkey may also falter.

ROMANTIC FREEDOM

While you are free-spirited, you are a firm believer in true love and work hard to make yours as sweet as it can be. However, you can be controlling at times and feel a little uncomfortable if your partner refuses to play ball. Try not to impose too much and allow your partner to act freely when they want to. You value your own personal freedom highly and should bear this in mind before committing to a relationship with another Horse-born. Having said this, a relationship with another Horse will bring you much affection and adventurous experiences, including travel to exciting places.

FRIENDS AND ALLIES

| TIGER | HORSE | DOG |

THE PERFECT MATCH — **SHEEP**

THE SHEEP

G entle and creative, the Sheep is the eighth animal in the Chinese zodiac. The number eight is a lucky number in Chinese culture because it symbolizes prosperity. This, along with the Sheep's gentle character, explains why it is among the most loved of animals everywhere.

SHEEP YEARS

1931, 1943, 1955, 1967, 1979, 1991, 2003, 2015, 2027, 2039

DATE RANGES FOR THE YEAR OF THE SHEEP

Start Date	End Date	Heavenly Stem	Earthly Branch
February 17, 1931	February 5, 1932	Metal	Earth
February 5, 1943	January 24, 1944	Water	Earth
January 24, 1955	February 11, 1956	Wood	Earth
February 9, 1967	January 30, 1968	Fire	Earth
January 28, 1979	February 15, 1980	Earth	Earth
February 15, 1991	February 3, 1992	Metal	Earth
February 1, 2003	January 21, 2004	Water	Earth
February 19, 2015	February 7, 2016	Wood	Earth
February 6, 2027	January 25, 2028	Fire	Earth
January 24, 2039	February 11, 2040	Earth	Earth

GENERAL CHARACTERISTICS

An elegant type, and highly accomplished in the arts, you are the most creative of all the signs. You have great fashion sense, and you are likely to be a designer or painter, or to work in the kind of profession where you can make the most of your gift for creating beautiful things. You tend to keep a quiet profile, but caught in the proper mood, you can be quite alive, humorous, and charming. When nurtured, these traits can make you an effective host or entertainer.

A wanderer by nature, you are happy to set off on a journey to meet new people and to see the world. You have a certain insecurity, however, and need to feel loved and protected. Although you are not innately materialistic, opportunities to make money seem to follow you. Be mindful of how you handle these opportunities, given your spendthrift ways. You likely face an uncertain future because of this habit. You can also be lazy sometimes; given the choice, you would definitely choose to marry a wealthy person and sit back for the rest of your life.

✳ SHEEP TYPES BY YEAR OF BIRTH

You will likely display one of five different personality types, based on your year of birth. The last number of your birth year determines your feng shui element, although you need to pay attention to the cutoff dates so you can determine your animal sign correctly. This is especially important if you were born in either January or February (see The Lunar Calendar, pages 12–13).

1 OR 2	↔	YOUR ELEMENT IS METAL	✛
3 OR 4	↔	YOUR ELEMENT IS WATER	🌊
5 OR 6	↔	YOUR ELEMENT IS WOOD	🌿
7 OR 8	↔	YOUR ELEMENT IS FIRE	🔥
9 OR 0	↔	YOUR ELEMENT IS EARTH	🟤

METAL SHEEP

1931 ▪ 1991

Endlessly creative, you are always looking for ways to add aesthetic value to your work. You love beautiful surroundings and find comfort in the company of friends and loved ones. You like to stick to old and familiar ways and have a tough time accepting changes. It is easier for you to accept new people into your circle if you see that they can be useful for you in the future. What others see as opportunism is to you just a good way to reach your goals.

WATER SHEEP

1943 ▪ 2003

A naturally caring and loyal person, you interact well with others because of your varied interests. You have an ear for music and love the arts. You work well with colleagues and superiors and are dedicated to your career. You are not the most adventurous type and resist sudden change. You sometimes have difficulty standing by your beliefs and are easily swayed by others. If this happens, you may find yourself being taken out of your comfort zone.

WOOD SHEEP

1955 ▪ 2015

You are the compassionate type that can always be trusted to help people in need. Such is your altruism that you are always on the lookout for those whose lives you can make better. A born diplomat, you are gifted with sociable traits that make you highly popular. You are very considerate and express yourself with utmost care lest you offend anyone. You may not realize it, but you can be a little overzealous in your desire to please others. Despite being ruled more by your heart than your head, you are prone to hiding your insecurities and tend to need the approval of others to feel complete.

FIRE SHEEP

1967 ▪ 2027

You are the flamboyant type who does not think twice about
spending more than necessary to keep a comfortable and beautiful
lifestyle. You have an outgoing personality, that sees you thrive
in social situations and you shine at both formal and informal
gatherings. A confident type, you can become so focused on yourself
that you disregard the feelings of others. You tend to approach
a task with a fair amount of drama and an attention to detail that
borders on the extreme, and this can cause tension between
you and your peers.

EARTH SHEEP

1979 ▪ 2039

Naturally optimistic, conscientious, and hugely independent, you
work well under pressure and encounter few difficulties career-wise.
Your cautious and prudent ways extend to handling your finances—
you may indulge your pleasures and those of your family, but you
are always in control of your expenditures. You are fiercely loyal to
your loved ones. You have rather strong opinions and can be brutally
frank; unfortunately, you are not open to criticism yourself
and tend to be defensive when at the receiving end
of negative feedback.

SHEEP TYPES BY MONTH OF BIRTH

Use the month of your birth to pinpoint your dominant personality type in a single word or phrase.

JANUARY	FEBRUARY	MARCH
Laid-back	Optimistic	Reticent
APRIL	**MAY**	**JUNE**
Thoughtful	Sensitive	Sophisticated
JULY	**AUGUST**	**SEPTEMBER**
Virtuous	Refined	Earnest
OCTOBER	**NOVEMBER**	**DECEMBER**
Unflappable	Eloquent	Kindhearted

FENG SHUI ADVICE

Our luck indications change every year, every month, and every day, and the best way to plot this is through the use of a reliable feng shui almanac. The following information is meant as a general guide for the Sheep.

	Lucky	Unlucky
Numbers	2, 7, 27	4, 9, 49, 94
Days	1st, 2nd, 8th of the month Success day*: Friday Vitality day**: Wednesday	5th, 20th, 25th of the month Unlucky day***: Thursday
Colors	Cream, beige, red, purple	Brown, pink, orange
Directions	North	Southwest
Flowers	Pink, apricot, and mixed carnations, primrose	

* SUCCESS DAY   This day is filled with positive energy and is considered lucky when planning important personal activities or social events.

** VITALITY DAY   This is the day when you are most active and vibrant.

*** UNLUCKY DAY   This day is considered inauspicious and you should avoid it when planning important personal activities or social events.

ZODIAC FACT

The Sheep is believed to be creative and gifted with great artistic talent. A quick look at some famous people born in the year of the Sheep gives credence to the claim. Frida Kahlo, Mark Twain, Julia Roberts, Robert De Niro, Ed Sheeran, Nat King Cole, Kurt Cobain, and George Harrison are among the many talented Sheep-born people.

YOUR CHARACTER STRENGTHS

Generally low profile, if you were born in the year of the Sheep, you are diligent and practical. When dealing with problems, you are not impulsive, and prefer to think things through very carefully. You do not care much about what others say and just do the things you deem right. You can be persistent and assertive but never arrogant. You prefer to live quietly, avoiding conflicts at all costs. Because you can be relied upon to complete a task left undone by others, you are valued as both friend and coworker.

Mild in nature, you are also polite, creative, and artistic. Inherently honest, you can trust that your judgment of others is fair and unbiased. Compassionate and sensitive to other people's feelings, you are quick to forgive or to help those in need. You know the value of saving for the future and do not squander money on flashy or unnecessary things.

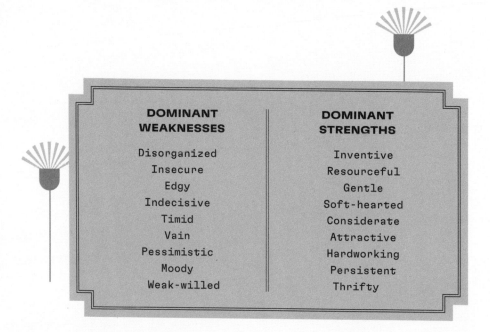

DOMINANT WEAKNESSES	DOMINANT STRENGTHS
Disorganized	Inventive
Insecure	Resourceful
Edgy	Gentle
Indecisive	Soft-hearted
Timid	Considerate
Vain	Attractive
Pessimistic	Hardworking
Moody	Persistent
Weak-willed	Thrifty

PERCEIVED WEAKNESSES

Something of a pessimist, you also believe strongly in destiny. You are shy and do not always find it easy to express your feelings. You try to avoid being the center of attention and would rather observe certain activities than actively participate in them.

You may appear calm, but deep inside you can be insecure and have the deepest need to be shown love and understanding. Prone to self-pity, you can be difficult to deal with. You will achieve more satisfaction in your personal relationships if you can overcome this weakness.

Because you are oftentimes indecisive, you are easily influenced by others. This indecisiveness is also seen by others as lack of drive and ambition, or sheer laziness. Your lack of self-confidence makes you vulnerable to being taken advantage of. Your mild and gentle demeanor has its downside and leaves you unable to handle stress properly—particularly as you tend to keep things to yourself. And because you tend deliberately not to criticize or displease friends and family members, you sometimes fail to make a stand on issues you hold dear.

PROSPECTS FOR YOUR CAREER

You like to take things slow and easy and tend to veer away from any form of negativity. You are generally pleasant, but dislike imposed norms and restrictions. Deep within yourself, you would rather not work alone, and in fact achieve greater things if you are part of a team.

CAREER OPTIONS

You are innately creative and gifted with an ear for music. A career in the theater or the arts suits you down to the ground. Outside of these fields, you do best when you are able to work with people who share your interests. Although seen as the silent type, when in the proper mood, you can be quite alive and charming, holding an audience with your wit and humor. If properly developed, these talents make you a great entertainer and effective party host. Essentially, you are deeply spiritual and have an original love for nature and natural things. A lover of pets, you thrive in the outdoors or in the natural habitat of animals. If sports interest you, you can become a remarkable athlete.

IN THE WORKPLACE

Given your wide-ranging creativity, you are not suited to fixed, scheduled desk jobs. You need recognition for your talents and encouragement to develop your skills. You thrive in jobs that involve close interaction with others, and should avoid positions that require you to work alone. If you have creative freedom in the workplace, you are a true inspiration to fellow team members. You are innovative and a logical thinker, both of which give you the potential to become a great inventor or engineer. With your prudence in handling money, you can start money-making ventures that will benefit many.

羊

PROSPECTS FOR DOMESTIC LIFE

You make an obedient child, a devoted partner, and a considerate parent. Warm and caring, you have many friends who enjoy being in your company. You are assured of the loyalty of your family members who are there to support you, despite your occasional stubbornness. Meticulous with your finances and spending, you find multiple ways in which to set something aside for the future. You just need to harmonize things through your creativity, and you are bound to enjoy a satisfying life.

HAPPY HOME

In raising your children, your character traits of tenderness and indecision both come to the fore. On the one hand, you charm your offspring into obedience without resorting to pressure, although this may involve trying to manipulate their feelings or persuading them with gifts and other rewards. On the other hand, you are not always successful in making your position on certain matters clear. This confuses your children, who are left to guess what you really want from them.

HOME STYLE

Elegance is your thing, and you like to be surrounded by beautiful objects. You adore variety, so each room in the home is likely to be different—be it in color or in the shapes and sizes of your furnishings. Your love of the outdoors is never far away. Your home has wide windows and plenty of them to allow natural light in. And you are not averse to getting your hands dirty with gardening. Back indoors, you avoid neutral colors as much as possible, and favor more of the fun and vibrant ones, or something that reminds you of the colors in your garden. You have plenty of live plants around for good measure.

FRIENDSHIP AND LOVE

With a mind focused on warm and fuzzy relationships, you enjoy nothing more than being with the people you love. Such a huge capacity for loving rewards you with several romantic liaisons in your youth. When you choose to settle down with the right person, you have the capacity to be an extremely loyal partner.

COMPATIBILITY

You thrive in the company of those born in the years of the Horse (your secret friend), the Boar, the Rabbit, and the Tiger. Both mild-mannered, you and a Rabbit achieve a very peaceful existence together. With the Boar, you share great creativity and are almost always in agreement with one another. A union with the Tiger is filled with respect and admiration and there is never room for boredom. You also make a great companion for another Sheep. You will find security with those born under the signs of the Horse, the Rabbit, and the Boar because you have complementary traits; where one is weak, the other can provide strength. The Dog, the Ox, and the Rat are your worst matches. You have trouble understanding each other's interests, which simply do not match.

IN THE LONG TERM

Kindhearted and family-oriented, you tend to fall in love more easily than others and with more than one person at a time, but you show true devotion when in a relationship and do your best to please a partner. Take care of your weaknesses, however. Your lack of self-confidence leads to you demanding constant attention from a partner, and you often make the situation worse, because you are not very open about your feelings. Those who find themselves in a romantic relationship with you have to be very understanding and supportive if the union is to stay harmonious.

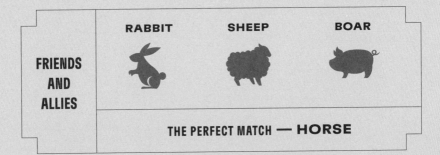

FRIENDS AND ALLIES

RABBIT **SHEEP** **BOAR**

THE PERFECT MATCH — HORSE

THE
MONKEY

The Monkey is the ninth animal in the Chinese zodiac order. People born under this sign are considered smart- and sharp-witted, though quite playful. In Chinese culture, Monkey years are popular choices for childbirth because it is believed that they will produce clever children.

MONKEY YEARS

1932, 1944, 1956, 1968, 1980, 1992, 2004, 2016, 2028, 2040

DATE RANGES FOR THE YEAR OF THE MONKEY

Start Date	End Date	Heavenly Stem	Earthly Branch
February 6, 1932	January 25, 1933	Water	Metal
January 25, 1944	February 12, 1945	Wood	Metal
February 12, 1956	January 30, 1957	Fire	Metal
January 30, 1968	February 16, 1969	Earth	Metal
February 16, 1980	February 4, 1981	Metal	Metal
February 4, 1992	January 22, 1993	Water	Metal
January 22, 2004	February 8, 2005	Wood	Metal
February 8, 2016	January 27, 2017	Fire	Metal
January 26, 2028	February 12, 2029	Earth	Metal
February 12, 2040	January 31, 2041	Metal	Metal

GENERAL CHARACTERISTICS

Inventive and charismatic, you are often the creative mind behind anything ingenious, including mischief. You have a natural quick-wittedness that enables you to grasp an ongoing situation as it unfolds and to make the right decision in dealing with it. In general, with your agile mind, deep desire for knowledge, and excellent memory, you can master any subject. This adds to your conversation skills and with your gift of gab, you wield strong influence and effectively engage your audience in sound discussions.

You can easily adapt to any situation and can be proficient in many types of jobs. You constantly seek fulfillment in your work and chase new and more exciting tasks. An adept problem-solver, you enjoy listening to your friends' problems and frequently help to ease them. On the down side, you are not great at hiding your feelings, and tend to wear your heart on your sleeve. Having said that, although you are strong willed, your anger is quick to cool.

✳ MONKEY TYPES BY YEAR OF BIRTH

You will likely display one of five different personality types, based on your year of birth. The last number of your birth year determines your feng shui element, although you need to pay attention to the cutoff dates so you can determine your animal sign correctly. This is especially important if you were born in either January or February (see The Lunar Calendar, pages 12–13).

0 OR 1	↔	YOUR ELEMENT IS METAL	✛
2 OR 3	↔	YOUR ELEMENT IS WATER	🌊
4 OR 5	↔	YOUR ELEMENT IS WOOD	🌿
6 OR 7	↔	YOUR ELEMENT IS FIRE	🔥
8 OR 9	↔	YOUR ELEMENT IS EARTH	◈

WATER MONKEY

1932 ▪ 1992

Always one to set clear goals, you do everything you can to achieve them, although you are flexible enough to adapt your methods while in pursuit of your objectives. Your clever ways, creativity, and amiable personality combine to draw support for your ideas, even though they may raise doubts at the start. You relate well to those around you and can be incredibly persuasive in getting others to do as you please. Friends and colleagues would do well to be aware of this, lest you manipulate them against their will. Take note that you are a sensitive type who does not respond well to criticism.

WOOD MONKEY

1944 ▪ 2004

While you have no problem gaining the respect of your colleagues, you tend to seek approval every now and then. Once assured of support, however, you can be counted on to be a loyal friend. You are driven by nature, and earnestly look for ways to improve a given situation if you are not happy with it. You are not one to sit still and love to learn new skills that will give you good results in the future. You are independent and can take care of yourself during difficult times. You have a perceptive mind and are a good judge of character.

FIRE MONKEY

1956 ▪ 2016

Competitive by nature, you have all the necessary qualities that make a good leader. Such potential can help get you to the top position and stay there. It can also make you a little overbearing at times, and you would do well to acknowledge your strong people skills, for you are adept at honing the talents of those working for you. A dominant type, take care that any activity or display of aggression does not become interpreted as jealousy of others.

EARTH MONKEY

1968 ▪ 2028

Honest and down-to-earth, unlike other Monkey types, you are not one to challenge convention. Consequently, you are perhaps the most stable among all your Monkey siblings. Studious and scholarly, you prefer to be in the background. However, this does not mean that you shun recognition of your achievements; you easily become discouraged if you do not get what you think you deserve. You are highly intelligent without being very vocal and others benefit from your wise thoughts.

METAL MONKEY

1980 ▪ 2040

Such is your independent and ambitious personality that you make a very good entrepreneur. Once you have set a goal, you are relentless in pursuing it through completion. Extremely focused, if you agree with directions set by others, you are an effective team player. You are never complacent and always look for creative ventures. With your gift of gab and persuasion, you make an excellent salesperson. You are good at handling your finances and secure your future early on.

MONKEY TYPES BY MONTH OF BIRTH

Use the month of your birth to pinpoint your dominant personality type in a single word or phrase.

JANUARY	FEBRUARY	MARCH
Pragmatic	Intelligent	Involved
APRIL	**MAY**	**JUNE**
Optimistic	Radial	Unpredictable
JULY	**AUGUST**	**SEPTEMBER**
Eloquent	Polite	Humble
OCTOBER	**NOVEMBER**	**DECEMBER**
Energetic	Dynamic	Cheerful

FENG SHUI ADVICE

Our luck indications change every year, every month, and every day, and the best way to plot this is through the use of a reliable feng shui almanac. The following information is meant as a general guide for the Monkey.

	Lucky	Unlucky
Numbers	4, 9, 49	2, 7, 27, 72
Days	1st, 2nd, 8th of the month Success day*: Friday Vitality day**: Thursday	9th, 10th, 17th of the month Unlucky day***: Tuesday
Colors	Gold, silver, white, yellow	Red, pink
Directions	Southwest, north, northwest, west	South, southeast
Flowers	Crape myrtle, chrysanthemum, "Ruby Prince" tulip	

* SUCCESS DAY   This day is filled with positive energy and is considered lucky when planning important personal activities or social events.

** VITALITY DAY   This is the day when you are most active and vibrant.

*** UNLUCKY DAY   This day is considered inauspicious and you should avoid it when planning important personal activities or social events.

FUN FACT

Some catchwords associated with the Monkey are clever, tricky, and artful. The term "monkey" affectionately refers to a child. It is also used in a derogatory manner to describe some adults. The idiomatic expression "monkeying around," which originated around the 1500s has been used to mean playing around with something in a careless and foolish way.

YOUR CHARACTER STRENGTHS

You have admirable capabilities and others are constantly amazed at your intense instinct and intuition. Whatever objectives you set for yourself, you pull out all the stops to accomplish them. With your keen interest in all things, you take a stab at even the slightest thing that intrigues you. Hugely active, you are always at the center of things, with a dynamism that allows you to use your personal resources to prevail day after day. You must be careful though, lest your energy gets spent. At any rate, even with such a handicap, you are a winner and so have the versatility required to start things over.

You are well known for being exceptionally affable and kind, and you consistently make an honest effort to help other people. Those around you respect you enormously and you are never without allies. You put a lot of energy and effort into looking great and your sense of humor is evident the moment you step into a group. You should be credited for your energy, and although you generally regard disappointments as simple learning experiences, rest assured, you are unlikely to see repeats of such events.

PERCEIVED WEAKNESSES

You are prone to take advantage of a situation in which you see an opportunity to bring in speedy cash or to outmaneuver an opponent. You might also be tempted to utilize your insight and beguiling nature to persuade others to join you in a venture, keeping them unwittingly unaware of any ulterior intentions you might have. In extreme cases, you can outmaneuver everybody, including yourself! Strangely, although you are always willing to offer advice and help others, such is your arrogance that you, yourself, disregard the advice of others and even decline offers of help. You are happy with your own endeavors and do not like to trouble friends, colleagues, or partners.

You are a ball of fire and are very disappointed if all your efforts fail to bring the outcome you have set your hopes on. You might even be difficult and hesitant to pay attention to the ideas of others. It does not take a lot for you to be happy; even small victories make you stick to how things are being run. Nevertheless, if you are not careful, you risk your lack of vision standing in the way of progress and success.

DOMINANT STRENGTHS	DOMINANT WEAKNESSES
Optimistic	Selfish
Enthusiastic	Self-indulgent
Self-assured	Jealous
Sociable	Suspicious
Innovative	Cunning
Inventive	Arrogant
Charismatic	Manipulative

PROSPECTS FOR YOUR CAREER

You are astute, adorable, and idealistic—characteristics that make for fruitful transactions and doing the unimaginable. Monkeys are hugely adaptable and you have a knack for appearing to be in charge at all times. You can adjust to any situation without difficulty and prove proficient in many types of occupations.

SUITABLE SITUATIONS

Full of energy, you are also persistently curious, which means you are always on the lookout for new learning experiences. Your ability to absorb a wide range of knowledge opens vast opportunities for you in many fields, including the performing arts, sports, teaching, and law. The world is your oyster, so to speak, but to succeed in any of those fields, you have to keep your interest and motivation in place. Since Monkeys are free spirits who hate restrictions in any form, you are best suited to freelance work, where you can give free rein to your energy and innovative ideas. Given the chance to work independently, you have more room to apply and further develop your wide range of talents.

CAREER STRENGTHS

Thoroughly agreeable, you make a great coworker and love to have a good time—you are frequently the bubbling energy source everyone crowds around. Used well, your excellent interpersonal skills make you highly influential. At work, those in senior positions notice your proposals and ideas for their soundness and effectiveness. You put a premium on finding pleasure in your work and, with your enthusiasm, you will likely complete tasks with high-quality results. Once the novelty wears off, however, you seek a shift or look for something new or more satisfying. Yearning for advancement is a great driving force and you are gifted with abilities that are useful in yielding higher income. You can be trusted to resolve complex situations, and where others are at a loss trying to find solutions, you always have a workable plan of action.

PROSPECTS FOR DOMESTIC LIFE

When it comes to home life, your parental responsibilities are a major priority. To you, children are the main reason for your existence. As a rule, it is an honor to fulfill your duties as a provider and nurturer. Just be mindful, however, that you could be driven by a need to be perceived as an ideal parent rather than by the deepest feelings of love for your offspring.

REARING CHILDREN

You always make a point of being involved in the activities of your children and welcome their friends into your home. It is at times like this that your cheerful and energetic personality comes into full play. You are never overly concerned with the ways of child rearing—your motto is the simpler things are, the better. As long as everybody feels good, you are happy to indulge your children's whims and give them good counsel. There is no room for boredom and you treat each day as if it is a holiday. You can sense if something is wrong with one of your young ones, or if something is troubling them. Having said that, you are not the most consistent of parents. With a busy mind and active social life, you may at times fail to deliver on a promised date or commitment with your kids which, of course, results in disappointment.

HOME STYLING

The Monkey is associated with the metal element and yang energy. As reflected in your home, this means that spaces are active and colorful. Most noticeable is the element of fun. It is not surprising to see funny or witty quotes captured in brightly colored frames, or in comical art pieces. Your movie collection includes a lot of comedies. Your love for the metal element can be seen in your chosen furniture and home accessories, which include metal furniture and decorative pieces that shimmer or glitter—think antique glass and lots of mirrors. For occasional peace and quiet, you need a water feature such as an aquarium or flowing water fountain to promote a reflective mood. Blue, gold, and white are your lucky colors and you tend to avoid drab neutral or earthy tones.

FRIENDSHIP AND LOVE

Among all the animal signs, you are the most admired for bringing joy into the lives of others. You are often witty and a good conversationalist, and people want you around at parties or social functions.

SUITABLE PARTNERS

The Rat, Dragon, and Snake are most compatible with you in a romantic sense—particularly the latter, as this is your secret friend. These animal signs also make good allies and partners in business. The Ox, Rabbit, Sheep, Horse, and Dog, also complement your character. Your optimism and glamor are lost on the Tiger, though. The compatibility wheel does not favor a Monkey and Boar romance, either. You may try to tolerate each other's eccentricities, but things may not be rosy.

FINDING BALANCE

You are not great at managing your own happiness. It takes a lot for friends and partners to make things work and too little to upset you. Your chosen partner needs patience to find balance in the relationship.

In both courtship and long-term relationships, you are sweet and loving. Many find themselves attracted to this. In turn, you are easily drawn to those who are happy-go-lucky and kind, like you. Before committing, you look at every aspect and scenario of a partnership, including child rearing and related responsibilities. Take care not to take too long on such reflection, as others may see this as an unwillingness to take the next big step.

Once you decide to take the plunge, your loyalty is unquestionable. You make an ideal partner and expect those you live with to be the same.

FRIENDS AND ALLIES	RAT	DRAGON	MONKEY

THE PERFECT MATCH — SNAKE

LEGEND

OF THE

TWELVE

ANIMALS

The Chinese zodiac remains an important aspect of traditional Chinese culture, and many legends exist surrounding the choice of animals that feature in it. The most popular story involves the legendary Jade Emperor who ruled the Heavens.

The story goes that the Jade Emperor organized a competition in which he invited all animals on Earth to cross from one side of a huge river to the other. The first twelve to make it across were to represent the years of a calendar being designed at the time.

Among the first to arrive at the starting line were the rat and the cat. Because they were poor swimmers, the two of them asked the ox if they could ride on its back. Midway through the race, the rat pushed the cat into the river, and the cat failed to complete the crossing. This is thought to be the reason why these two animals are such fierce enemies to this day.

As the ox approached the far bank of the river, the rat jumped off to become the first animal to finish the race. Behind the rat were the ox, the tiger, and the rabbit. The dragon came in fifth—it could have done better because of its ability to fly, but was held back because it helped the meek rabbit make it to the shore. The snake and the horse finished sixth and seventh, respectively. The sheep, the monkey, and the rooster helped each other during the race and were given the eighth, ninth, and tenth places.

The dog, despite being a good swimmer finished in eleventh place because it took its sweet time to get a good bath. Finally, the boar, after taking a nap, became the twelfth and last animal to make the crossing, so completing the zodiac cycle.

These animals have remained in use since time was officially recorded during the reign of Emperor Huang Ti, around 2637 BCE. Every year is assigned an animal and the cycle repeats itself in this particular order: Rat, Ox, Tiger, Rabbit, Dragon, Snake, Horse, Sheep, Monkey, Rooster, Dog, and Boar.

THE
ROOSTER

The Rooster, the tenth animal sign in the Chinese zodiac, symbolizes confidence and intelligence. Decisive and outspoken, this zodiac sign is also most commonly associated with power, courage, benevolence, and trustworthiness.

ROOSTER YEARS

1933, 1945, 1957, 1969, 1981, 1993, 2005, 2017, 2029, 2041

DATE RANGES FOR THE YEAR OF THE ROOSTER

Start Date	End Date	Heavenly Stem	Earthly Branch
January 26, 1933	February 13, 1934	Water	Metal
February 13, 1945	February 1, 1946	Wood	Metal
January 31, 1957	February 17, 1958	Fire	Metal
February 17, 1969	February 5, 1970	Earth	Metal
February 5, 1981	January 24, 1982	Metal	Metal
January 23, 1993	February 9, 1994	Water	Metal
February 9, 2005	January 28, 2006	Wood	Metal
January 28, 2017	February 15, 2018	Fire	Metal
February 13, 2029	February 2, 2030	Earth	Metal
February 1, 2041	January 21, 2042	Metal	Metal

GENERAL CHARACTERISTICS

Often a little eccentric, you have difficult relationships with others. You tend to think that you are always right and usually you are! You can be selfish and too outspoken, but you are always engaging and can be extremely brave.

Actively interested in clothes, colors, and accessories, you can be very critical about your own appearance and about that of others. You like to be noticed and flattered. You may be criticized for being boastful, but the compassion and wisdom that come to the fore when others need help make up for this deficiency.

In pursuing what you want in life, you may face blocks that wear you down. With your firm resolve, however, you are able to rebound quickly. You are pragmatic, yet you dream far and are brave enough to go after your life goals. You feel uneasy when you learn that other people are curious about your personal affairs and will find it hard to take criticisms lightly. You have little room for pettiness, which adds to your enviable self-confidence.

✻ ROOSTER TYPES BY YEAR OF BIRTH

You will likely display one of five different personality types, based on your year of birth. The last number of your birth year determines your feng shui element, although you need to pay attention to the cutoff dates so you can determine your animal sign correctly. This is especially important if you were born in either January or February (see The Lunar Calendar, pages 12–13).

1 OR 2	↔	YOUR ELEMENT IS METAL	✛
3 OR 4	↔	YOUR ELEMENT IS WATER	🦢
5 OR 6	↔	YOUR ELEMENT IS WOOD	🌿
7 OR 8	↔	YOUR ELEMENT IS FIRE	🔥
9 OR 0	↔	YOUR ELEMENT IS EARTH	◆

WATER ROOSTER

1933 ▪ 1993

Smart- and quick-witted, you are adept at coming up with quick solutions to even very difficult situations. Career-wise, you have no problem drawing support from those above you and cooperation from fellow colleagues. You are calm but highly sensitive and proud. Though you have an eye for artistic things, you are not one to show off your achievements and acquisitions. Take care not to offend others with your overly frank and direct way of expressing your thoughts.

WOOD ROOSTER

1945 ▪ 2005

Sociable and willing to do anything for friends, you love company and put prime importance on family matters. In a crowd, you are almost always the one cracking jokes and easing tension. You are prone to being overly dependent on those around you—try to be more patient and persevering in easing your problems rather than relying on others. You are also somewhat given to fantasy and need to balance the tendency to have too many dreams. Careful and scrupulous with details, you run the risk of others finding your standards rather steep.

FIRE ROOSTER

1957 ▪ 2017

A born leader, you are smart, confident, and enterprising, and thrive in competitive situations. You push for challenging work rather than humdrum jobs and enjoy great career success. You seek constant stimulation in the workplace and become short-tempered when you cannot complete a given task on time. You are rather impatient, always feeling that there is something missing if you don't get things done. Highly independent, you value your privacy and may find yourself shunning intimacy.

EARTH ROOSTER

1969 ▪ 2029

The most active of the five Rooster types, you like to travel and make new friends. Pragmatic at work, you draw from past experiences to solve present problems while exercising the utmost patience and perseverance at all times. Prone to being proud, you may not be too open to the opinions of others, and this can be a hindrance at times. Still, your career runs smoothly because of your hard work and the support of your superiors. Charming in nature, you are bound to enjoy a happy romantic life. You also have good wealth luck as you have a strong ability to create income.

METAL ROOSTER

1981 ▪ 2041

Independent and determined, you stand firm during adverse situations and do not give up easily. You are reliable and prove your true worth as a friend in times of trouble. You tend to be stubborn, however, and do not go into something without a clear purpose. You are a keen observer. Gifted with good communication skills, you work harmoniously with others and excel in jobs that put your negotiating power to practical use. Take care as you climb the ladder, however, as your strong personality may surface, turning others off who perceive you as tough and hard to please.

ROOSTER TYPES BY MONTH OF BIRTH

Use the month of your birth to pinpoint your dominant personality type in a single word or phrase.

JANUARY	FEBRUARY	MARCH
Watchful	Freedom-loving	Noble
APRIL	**MAY**	**JUNE**
Carefree	Diligent	Sensitive
JULY	**AUGUST**	**SEPTEMBER**
Impetuous	Individualistic	Fearless
OCTOBER	**NOVEMBER**	**DECEMBER**
Incorruptible	Fair	Inspirational

FENG SHUI ADVICE

Our luck indications change every year, every month, and every day, and the best way to plot this is through the use of a reliable feng shui almanac. The following information is meant as a general guide for the Rooster.

	Lucky	Unlucky
Numbers	5, 7, 8, 57, 58	1, 3, 9, 13, 19
Days	7th, 14th, 25th of the month Success day*: Friday Vitality day**: Thursday	3rd, 11th, 24th of the month Unlucky day***: Tuesday
Colors	Brown, white, gold, yellow	Red, pink, purple, orange
Directions	West, south, southeast	East
Flowers	Celosia, cockscomb, glamini dwarf gladiolus	

* SUCCESS DAY   This day is filled with positive energy and is considered lucky when planning important personal activities or social events.

** VITALITY DAY   This is the day when you are most active and vibrant.

*** UNLUCKY DAY   This day is considered inauspicious and you should avoid it when planning important personal activities or social events.

FUN FACT

There is one thing about the Rooster that cannot be said about any other Chinese zodiac animal, and that is: the outline of a rooster reflects the shape of China on the map! This is just one of the many reasons why it is a much-loved animal sign that has become associated with good fortune.

YOUR CHARACTER STRENGTHS

A social type, you are in your element when making new acquaintances at parties and celebrations. Moreover, you are a fantastic party host yourself, going out of your way to please your guests. Your social circle is likely to include friends from a range of different fields because Roosters enjoy all types of personalities.

People might describe you as opinionated, friendly, and very talented. You are particularly loved for your honesty and compassionate spirit, and you often feel strongly about humanitarian and environmental causes. Reading is a particular passion of yours, and you can engage anyone in intellectual discourse. Moreover, you are a profound philosopher, are critical, and very few things get past you without scrutiny. You tend to think you are correct about things, which can come across as boastful, but it almost always turns out to be true.

Your pleasure-loving character and spirit ensure that you leave an excellent lasting impression on the people you encounter. You have high ambitions—take care not to let them threaten relationships with those around you. Success in this respect sees your creative ideas benefitting many.

DOMINANT STRENGTHS	DOMINANT WEAKNESSES
Truthful	Perfectionist
Sensible	Gullible
Independent	Impatient
Capable	Critical
Compassionate	Eccentric
Quick-minded	Narrow-minded
Philosophical	Selfish

雞

PERCEIVED
WEAKNESSES

You are prone to thinking a little too highly of yourself. During intellectual discussions, you often show little regard for views other than your own and are capable of being brutally frank and tactless. You rarely tolerate pettiness. Take care as, unfortunately, such self-confidence comes across as arrogance if you are not careful.

You are transparent about your ideas and are so driven that you cannot control yourself at times; you often say things you are sorry for later. In addition, you make a fuss over minor things and are easily distracted. This sees you spend much time on trivial things while depriving yourself of the chance to focus on more meaningful matters. Although you can be sensitive at times, you cannot be faulted for your honesty and reliability.

While pragmatic, you dream far and are brave enough to run after what you want in life. Anything that threatens to block your dreams gets you down, but you are usually able to rebound quickly. You find it hard to take criticism and show uneasiness when you discover other people prying into your personal affairs.

雞

PROSPECTS FOR YOUR CAREER

You always have creative ideas to contribute to a team. You are quick to grasp key points, good at observing others, and are very enthusiastic at doing your tasks. Highly adaptable to every situation, early in your career you have many opportunities to develop your talents and are recognized for your input. Sustained by your youthful ambition, you enjoy a successful career with a good income.

CAREER HIGHS

It seems that whatever profession you choose, you excel because of your boundless enthusiasm. You may opt to be in the entertainment field where natural eloquence, wit, and social skills come to the fore. If you are not to be the entertainer yourself, you make an excellent coach for would-be celebrities on account of your persuasive communication and management skills.

You have artistic inclinations and love to be the center of attention. Such creativity makes you suitable for jobs that require a keen eye for detail and style. Highly organized, you always have your to-do lists ready. You are good at handling finances and saving money; a shortage of cash is unlikely to be an issue for you. Despite the promise of a stable career, you may not want to be an employee all your life and might aspire to becoming a business owner. With your foresight and clever mind, this is not entirely impossible—you have lucky prospects and there is always a reliable ally to render assistance.

FORCEFUL PERSONALITY

For all your drive, ambition, and prudence with handling money, you have a vain side that sees you showing off and being ruled by your pleasure-seeking nature. Because you can sometimes be impatient and rigid about certain things, you may not be the best choice for a leadership position. Your independent personality can catch others off guard. You do not hold back with your thoughts and readily disregard the opinions of others; still, your pleasing personality gains you respect. You may not be the most tactful of people, but you are forthright and loyal.

PROSPECTS FOR DOMESTIC LIFE

Loyal to a partner, you aspire to having a large family. You are not great with children but can be conscientious, even if somewhat authoritarian. It is a priority for you to secure the best possible education for your offspring.

PARENTING SKILLS

You are a very responsible parent and are ready to make any sacrifice for the sake of your children. Take care that they do not see through this weakness and use it to their advantage. You certainly expect respect from the young ones and should a child show any form of rebellion or differences in ways and opinions, it surprises you and you do not take it well. You have little or no room for disagreements—any form of conflict makes you feel lost and in much pain.

TYPICAL LIFESTYLE

You are adept at juggling many things—so much so that others wonder how you can be so successful. Opinionated and vocal, you may come across as dominating. You dress in ways that make you look smart without being flamboyant. Your classy taste, which shows in your well-appointed home, is the envy of many. You want your home to be serious and sensible in most respects. You like private spaces in which you can feel safe and protected and do everything you can to live in a property where you and your family feel secure.

Being a yin animal, your home features many metal and water elements. Your style is generally conservative, with comfortable furniture and low lighting conducive to reading and restful activities. Colors are predominantly warm, with gold, yellow, and brown lending a laid-back fall feeling. After all, that is the season that reminds you of happy times when you can look back at reaping what you have sown. You are determined to succeed in life, and a home that allows you to take a step back and relax is your idea of rewarding yourself after all your hard work.

FRIENDSHIP AND LOVE

You are among the animal signs who are lucky in love. People born in a Rooster year are courageous, easygoing, and passionate. In life and in love, you crave attention and praise from others and especially your partners. You know when the feelings are real and only respond to those whose intentions are sincere.

YOUR BEST MATCHES

People born in the year of the Rooster are ideally matched with those born in the year of the Dragon—their secret friend—the Ox, and the Snake. You will never have a dull moment with an Ox. With the Snake and the Dragon, the compatibility score gets even higher owing to their many complementary characteristics. You find those born in the years of the Sheep, the Boar, the Rat, and the Tiger supportive. Unfortunately, while another Rooster makes for a great ally, romance has dim prospects. Your personalities are so dominant that you are likely unwilling to yield to one another. You find the Monkey too evasive and the Dog overly guarded.

HIGHS AND LOWS

You are a smart dresser—always well-groomed—which makes you irresistible to prospective partners. It helps, too, that you have that vibrant energy and an optimistic outlook on life. You are such a free spirit that you are likely to be in more than one relationship at one time. Love means a lot to you, and although you can be flirtatious at first, you will only pursue a relationship that you see as having real potential. Once in, you are loyal to the core, working hard on the union and taking very good care of your partner.

With your charming and romantic nature, you want your relationships to last. Your only hurdle is the fact that you have rather strong feelings about people; you either like or dislike them and there is no middle ground. This can make romance and intimacy difficult to maintain. Also, you can be controlling and will tend to argue over minor things. Your pride, and sometimes misplaced self-esteem, threaten to jeopardize your efforts to build harmonious relationships. If only you could manage these weaknesses, you would have a better chance of making the perfect partnership.

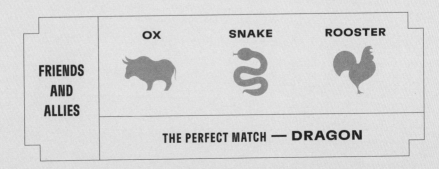

FRIENDS AND ALLIES

OX **SNAKE** **ROOSTER**

THE PERFECT MATCH — DRAGON

THE
DOG

Taking the eleventh place in the Chinese zodiac, the Dog is the ultimate symbol of loyalty and honesty. In both Eastern and Western cultures, it is considered human's best friend owing to its steadfast loyalty to humans.

DOG YEARS

1934, 1946, 1958, 1970, 1982, 1994, 2006, 2018, 2030, 2042

DATE RANGES FOR THE YEAR OF THE DOG

Start Date	End Date	Heavenly Stem	Earthly Branch
February 14, 1934	February 3, 1935	Wood	Earth
February 2, 1946	January 21, 1947	Fire	Earth
February 18, 1958	February 7, 1959	Earth	Earth
February 6, 1970	January 26, 1971	Metal	Earth
January 25, 1982	February 12, 1983	Water	Earth
February 10, 1994	January 30, 1995	Wood	Earth
January 29, 2006	February 17, 2007	Fire	Earth
February 16, 2018	February 4, 2019	Earth	Earth
February 3, 2030	January 22, 2031	Metal	Earth
January 22, 2042	February 9, 2043	Water	Earth

GENERAL
CHARACTERISTICS

You have a deep sense of loyalty, are honest, and inspire confidence in others because you know how to keep a secret. An idealist and a dreamer to the core, you never really accept the fact that injustice and oppression can exist in the world.

Others often fail to see your insightful side, which borders at times on being cynical and pessimistic. You tend to imagine things that could possibly go wrong around you. This causes you undue anxiety and stress, especially if you feel that you may not be of any help during those situations. On the other hand, you are very supportive of those who are loyal to you. You are an altruistic soul and do not think twice about using your available resources to help others.

With your strong sense of duty and responsibility, you make a good leader, but you should learn to relax and realize that it is impossible to control everything. You can be cold emotionally and sometimes distant socially. You also have a tendency to find fault with many things and are noted for your sharp tongue.

狗

✻ DOG TYPES BY YEAR OF BIRTH

You will likely display one of five different personality types, based on your year of birth. The last number of your birth year determines your feng shui element, although you need to pay attention to the cutoff dates so you can determine your animal sign correctly. This is especially important if you were born in either January or February (see The Lunar Calendar, pages 12–13).

0 OR 1	↔	YOUR ELEMENT IS METAL	✛
2 OR 3	↔	YOUR ELEMENT IS WATER	🜄
4 OR 5	↔	YOUR ELEMENT IS WOOD	🜔
6 OR 7	↔	YOUR ELEMENT IS FIRE	🜂
8 OR 9	↔	YOUR ELEMENT IS EARTH	🜃

WOOD DOG

1934 ▪ 1994

Honest, dependable, and mild-mannered—especially in your speech—you have a strong sense of justice and make a stand against unfair practices, rarely backing down until apologies are said. You are genuinely grateful for the favors and support that come your way and try to show your appreciation in various ways. You are persistent and enjoy many worthwhile experiences in the workplace. You are not one for extravagance and tend to haggle before making a purchase of any kind. Others may find this objectionable, but this is your key to an easy and comfortable life later on.

FIRE DOG

1946 ▪ 2006

Known to be gentle and kind, you have the opportunity to create
a bright future for yourself. You will likely fulfill your dreams, not
because you are so driven but because your ideals are not that
high. Loyal and generous, you are easily controlled in a relationship.
When asked for help by friends who might be in trouble, you are
sympathetic but do not extend a hand without analyzing the
situation. When it comes to love, you express your feelings
in a very direct manner, which may be seen as unromantic.

EARTH DOG

1958 ▪ 2018

Highly principled, you stand by your actions and the decisions you
make. This sometimes manifests as you saying what is on your mind
and doing as you think, which can inadvertently offend some people.
This is an unfortunate trait, as you never intend to hurt others.
You do not like to meddle in the lives of those around you, and cannot
stand any form of interference in yours. You may not be the best
at creating a romantic atmosphere, but you certainly give all you
have for your loved ones and are very faithful.

METAL DOG

1970 ▪ 2030

Highly independent, you prefer to rely on your own efforts
rather than seek help from others. You are a conscientious worker
and because of your prudent spending, you find yourself financially
secure later in life. You also enjoy great security in whatever
work you do because you do not think twice about helping others
to finish certain tasks. You make a good politician and are likely
to be blessed with good luck at the height of your career.
You handle your finances well and prefer simple living that
allows you to save for the future.

WATER DOG

1982 ▪ 2042

Generally, and with the help of benefactors and mentor figures, you
experience smooth sailing in life. You may have to work hard in your
youth, with your luck improving later in life. You are the late bloomer
among all the Dog types. Serious and responsible in your job, you
may stay at one workplace for a long while. You are a good money
manager and plan your purchases well. But take care: while you
can make money easily, you may only be cut out for a stable income
rather than any great fortune. Your romantic liaisons would improve
with better communication.

DOG TYPES BY MONTH OF BIRTH

Use the month of your birth to pinpoint your dominant personality type in a single word or phrase.

JANUARY	FEBRUARY	MARCH
Deliberate	Adventurous	Realistic
APRIL	**MAY**	**JUNE**
Ambitious	Honest	Extravagant
JULY	**AUGUST**	**SEPTEMBER**
Optimistic	Analytical	Versatile
OCTOBER	**NOVEMBER**	**DECEMBER**
Pleasant	Lively	Trustworthy

FENG SHUI ADVICE

Our luck indications change every year, every month, and every day, and the best way to plot this is through the use of a reliable feng shui almanac. The following information is meant as a general guide for the Dog.

	Lucky	Unlucky
Numbers	3, 4, 9, 34, 39	1, 6, 7, 16, 17
Days	5th, 9th, 27th of the month Success day*: Monday Vitality day**: Wednesday	3rd, 11th, 12th of the month Unlucky day***: Thursday
Colors	Purple, beige, cream, red	White, blue, gold
Directions	Northwest, east, south, northeast	Southeast
Flowers	"Middleton Valley" rose, orchid, cymbidium	

* SUCCESS DAY   This day is filled with positive energy and is considered lucky when planning important personal activities or social events.

** VITALITY DAY   This is the day when you are most active and vibrant.

*** UNLUCKY DAY   This day is considered inauspicious and you should avoid it when planning important personal activities or social events.

FENG SHUI FACT

In ancient China, dogs were used in more practical ways as transporters of goods, rather than as human companions. Today, dog images are used as protection and luck symbols in many Chinese homes and establishments. Black poodles are most popular because they are particularly associated with good luck.

YOUR CHARACTER STRENGTHS

If you were born in the year of the Dog, you are typically down-to-earth and straightforward. Faithful, courageous, nimble, and kindhearted, you are discreet and can be trusted to keep secrets, which earns you the confidence of your friends and colleagues. You make a good leader.

Observant and perceptive, you can assess the character of someone you have just met simply by noting how they look and express themselves. You hold back and do not verbalize your impressions, however, lest they lead to a misunderstanding. You manage your feelings well and can be very discerning. You know when to let simple misgivings pass, so you are always welcome in any group.

You have a thirst for learning and do not stop until you have mastered a certain subject before starting a new one. Seeing things through to completion is a very positive trait and you rarely leave anything half done. A quick thinker, you keep your cool, even under pressure. And on the rare occasions that you lose your temper, it never lasts very long. The expression "you cannot teach an old dog new tricks" unravels when it comes to failure. Instead of being bogged down by missteps, you use them as lessons and opportunities to relearn or improve on your past efforts.

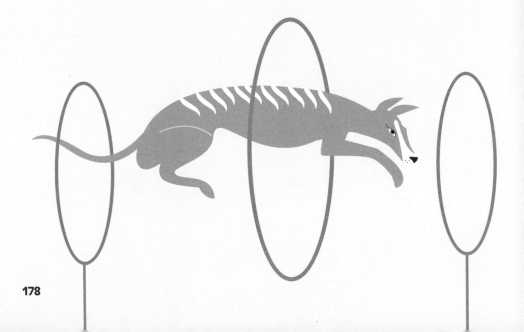

PERCEIVED WEAKNESSES

You may appear energetic and lively on the outside, but deep inside you are insightful and even a little cynical and pessimistic. You tend to imagine scenarios in which things go wrong around you. In your mind, you are quick to form theories that have no basis in fact. This causes you undue anxiety and excessive worry, especially if you feel that a given situation is beyond your help.

You hold very strong opinions and are slow to trust others. Once you do, however, you are fiercely loyal. Having your trust betrayed is another matter entirely—you have no qualms about giving the offending party a dose of their own medicine. Often driven to extremes, you seldom take the middle ground and rarely change your established views on anyone; thus, it is important that others make a good first impression on contact with you.

Though generally appealing, you can be cold emotionally and sometimes aloof. Quick to find faults in others, you can be rather sharp-tongued. A tendency toward irritability makes you anxious for no reason, although you always take the time to calm down and regain your composure.

DOMINANT STRENGTHS	DOMINANT WEAKNESSES
Loyal	Inflexible
Sensitive	Volatile
Responsible	Oversensitive
Clever	Conservative
Courageous	Stubborn
Lively	Emotional
Perceptive	Cynical

PROSPECTS FOR YOUR CAREER

With your naturally warm personality, you are a perfect fit for jobs that require interpersonal skills. Your strong service orientation makes you ideal for social welfare, education, law, or medical professions. You need the proper motivation to maximize your inherent strengths, however. Without it, you lack inner drive and tend to go with the flow, and this may prevent you from achieving your goals.

IN THE WORKPLACE

Always a source of insightful suggestions, you are invaluable in positions assisting the decision makers. As a leader, you are driven by your own strengths and use them as a guide when choosing employees. You have no trouble filling up certain job positions with the ideal candidates with appropriate skills. You are a great problem solver and do not shy away from competitive activities, which makes you more alive and in your element.

Thanks to your charm, you always win the support of your coworkers, superiors, or business partners. As a colleague, you can be counted on to extend help when needed. You do this not simply because you can or with an eye on the potential reward, but because you expect to learn something valuable from your efforts. With this mindset of easing off other people's load, you can expect to do well as a counselor, teacher, and justice or religious worker.

CAREER PROSPECTS

Early in your working life, although you may lack experience, you have great ideas and suggestions. All you need is a capable mentor to help you develop your skills. You are earnest in doing your job and do not give up easily, despite any challenges you may face. Consequently, you experience upward movement and job stability early on. Throughout your working life, chances arise in which you can seize proper opportunities for growth and promotion— or expansion if you choose to go into business. With your honesty and optimism, career satisfaction follows you everywhere. However, you need to guard against careless spending to avoid financial disaster. Be mindful about investing your hard-earned money on untested businesses.

PROSPECTS FOR DOMESTIC LIFE

Far from being materialistic, you derive the greatest pleasure from your family and loved ones. An altruistic soul, you prefer to use your available resources to help others. As long as you are able to support family members and enjoy the occasional luxury with them, you feel satisfied.

FAMILY LIFE

You are most comfortable in small, intimate get-togethers where you can enjoy meaningful conversations with family and friends. In such small groups, others enjoy your company too, and are held captive by your interesting insights and stories. Your honesty and down-to-earth nature surfaces in those gatherings.

Prone to sentimentality, you are temporarily weakened by problems and tragedies in the family. This is not long-lasting, however, and you always find ways to overcome such difficulties. When it comes to your children, you are a good role model and their most loyal friend and protector. Your world revolves around their welfare—from providing for their needs, guiding and disciplining them while they are young, and watching them build their own lives, you perform your duties with the utmost dedication.

A DOG'S HOME

Highly organized, you cannot stand mess, so it is important for you to have a home that is well kept and neat. Everything has its proper place. You do not shy away from doing your part in the household chores—a reflection of your need to be active and useful. You are highly territorial and your desire for personal space sometimes causes conflict among family members. Every space and each room in your house must have a practical purpose, and luxury is out of the question. You have a tendency to spend money on unnecessary things and do not have an eye for making profitable investments. This unwise purchasing should be kept in check if you want to avoid financial problems later on.

FRIENDSHIP AND LOVE

While it is true that trustworthiness is one of your best qualities, you find it difficult to give that trust to others. Thus, initially, you may either be quick to judge or take your time before being at ease in the company of people you have just met.

GOOD PAIRINGS

In love and romance, as long as your personal space and time are not needlessly intruded on, there is harmony. The Tiger, Horse, or another Dog make the greatest friends and allies because of your strong compatibility as free spirits. Relationships with Horses are lasting because you share mutual trust. The brave Tiger boosts your confidence in meeting life challenges. You will find the best match in your secret friend, the Rabbit. You are least compatible with the Dragon because you are both headstrong. The dreamy Sheep, the outspoken Rooster, and the stubborn Ox are not ideal matches either.

LOVE TRAITS

Your tendency not to trust others gets in the way of building meaningful relationships. Would-be partners sense this insecurity and choose to keep their distance. This is unfortunate because, while you can be cautious, you are very loyal in love. In fact, you are possibly the most loyal lover among all zodiac signs. Once given the chance to see your romantic strengths, your partner has every reason to feel secure. They still need to be wary of your fragile emotional makeup, however, as the slightest act of betraying your trust leads to unwanted consequences.

FRIENDS AND ALLIES	TIGER	HORSE	DOG

THE PERFECT MATCH — RABBIT

THE
BOAR

The Boar is the last of the twelve animal signs in the Chinese zodiac, and is associated with retirement and relaxation. Generous and tolerant, boars are happy and optimistic beings who enjoy life's physical pleasures.

BOAR YEARS

1935, 1947, 1959, 1971, 1983, 1995, 2007, 2019, 2031, 2043

DATE RANGES FOR THE YEAR OF THE BOAR

Start Date	End Date	Heavenly Stem	Earthly Branch
February 4, 1935	January 23, 1936	Wood	Water
January 22, 1947	February 9, 1948	Fire	Water
February 8, 1959	January 27, 1960	Earth	Water
January 27, 1971	February 14, 1972	Metal	Water
February 13, 1983	February 1, 1984	Water	Water
January 30, 1995	February 18, 1996	Wood	Water
February 17, 2007	February 6, 2008	Fire	Water
February 4, 2019	January 24, 2020	Earth	Water
January 22, 2031	February 10, 2032	Metal	Water
February 10, 2043	January 29, 2044	Water	Water

GENERAL CHARACTERISTICS

Highly intelligent and with a heart of gold, you are probably the most generous among the zodiac signs, believing that all people are basically good. Sadly, this trait leaves you open to others less generous taking advantage of you. You also tend to see things through rose-colored glasses; no matter how bad a problem seems to be, you try to work it out, honestly if sometimes impulsively. A lover of nature, you are happiest when you are out somewhere, far from the city. You constantly sacrifice your own happiness and comfort for the sake of your loved ones. You love luxury and have impeccable manners.

You are the touchy-feely type who is open about showing your affection. Spending time with friends and family is what makes you happy. Being the acknowledged peacemaker in the Chinese zodiac does not mean you have a weak character. Quite the contrary, you are very straightforward and will speak only the truth. You cannot stand any form of hypocrisy and deception. Given your strong convictions, you are very reasonable and will easily forgive those who have done you wrong—no grudges, no ill feelings, no intent to exact revenge. Kindness is ingrained in your DNA.

豬

✱ BOAR TYPES BY YEAR OF BIRTH

You will likely display one of five different personality types, based on your year of birth. The last number of your birth year determines your feng shui element, although you need to pay attention to the cutoff dates so you can determine your animal sign correctly. This is especially important if you were born in either January or February (see The Lunar Calendar, pages 12–13).

1 OR 2	↔	YOUR ELEMENT IS METAL	✛
3 OR 4	↔	YOUR ELEMENT IS WATER	🌊
5 OR 6	↔	YOUR ELEMENT IS WOOD	🌿
7 OR 8	↔	YOUR ELEMENT IS FIRE	🔥
9 OR 0	↔	YOUR ELEMENT IS EARTH	✿

WOOD BOAR

1935 ▪ 1995

The warmth of the wood contributes to you having a personality that is kind and giving and at the same time rather complex. Compassionate in spirit, you are a valuable team member who is driven by the spirit of cooperation on a deeper level than just social. This makes you welcome in professions that require solid teamwork. The negative implication of this is, of course, that you may overcommit to doing tasks beyond your capacity. You have a friendly attitude with a good sense of humor, and can be very persuasive.

FIRE BOAR

1947 ▪ 2007

Fire is a symbol of dynamism and courage and you are gifted with these traits. You have greater initiative than other Boar types, who tend to go with the flow. Highly motivated and full of energy, you can find yourself working simultaneously on different initiatives but do not lose the stamina to see them through. You are also an assertive type and hold your ground despite tough opposition, leaving it to the other person to yield. As a more ambitious type of Boar, you stand a good chance of succeeding in your chosen field.

EARTH BOAR

1959 ▪ 2019

Practical and down-to-earth, you know better than to be compelled to do things that are next to impossible or too idealistic. Socially active, you have a large circle of friends of all kinds and are recognized for your good sense of humor and eloquence in speaking. You shy away from confrontations, but are open to practical experiences that could help you in the future. This will contribute vastly to your chances for success—although this is not something you would choose to boast about. Loving and sensual, you also lean toward being mysterious.

METAL BOAR

1971 ▪ 2031

In general, you are kind and compliant to all—so much so that you can be passive and naive and others may take advantage of you. However, the metal element in your character makes you strong and determined. Once betrayed, you readily put offenders in their place. You are, perhaps, the most ambitious among the Boars and use this drive not only to do whatever pleases you, but also to contribute to worthwhile causes. Very persevering, you will continue to work with passion even after others have given up.

WATER BOAR

1983 ▪ 2043

A sociable being, you go out of your way to make others comfortable and at home. You are compassionate and understanding to all those you consider to be your friends and even extend this generosity to complete strangers. Once you feel secure in a relationship, you go all out in showing your loving persona. On the downside, you are prone to looking at your partner's desire for space and freedom as a sign of rejection and feel anxious as a result. You place a high value on security and intimacy in relationships.

BOAR TYPES BY MONTH OF BIRTH

Use the month of your birth to pinpoint your dominant personality type in a single word or phrase.

JANUARY	FEBRUARY	MARCH
Sincere	Frugal	Emotional
APRIL	**MAY**	**JUNE**
Motivated	Independent	Sentimental
JULY	**AUGUST**	**SEPTEMBER**
Indolent	Energetic	Finicky
OCTOBER	**NOVEMBER**	**DECEMBER**
Hopeful	Obstinate	Decisive

FENG SHUI ADVICE

Our luck indications change every year, every month, and every day, and the best way to plot this is through the use of a reliable feng shui almanac. The following information is meant as a general guide for the Boar.

	Lucky	Unlucky
Numbers	2, 5, 8, 25, 58	1, 7, 17, 71
Days	2nd, 8th, 11th of the month Success day*: Wednesday Vitality day**: Tuesday	3rd, 12th, 16th of the month Unlucky day***: Saturday
Colors	Yellow, gray, brown, gold	Red, blue, green
Directions	Northwest, east, southwest	Southeast
Flowers	Endless summer hydrangea, gerbera daisy	

* SUCCESS DAY
This day is filled with positive energy and is considered lucky when planning important personal activities or social events.

** VITALITY DAY
This is the day when you are most active and vibrant.

*** UNLUCKY DAY
This day is considered inauspicious and you should avoid it when planning important personal activities or social events.

FENG SHUI FACT

Since ancient times, boars have come to represent wealth and good luck. Many theories have it that piggy banks originated during the Qing dynasty in China. The round or chubby face and long ears of this pig symbol are believed to attract income luck.

YOUR CHARACTER STRENGTHS

A straightforward type, you speak only of the truth. You are highly conversant and can communicate well. You hate any form of hypocrisy and deception since you firmly believe in fair treatment, justice, and law. Given your strong convictions, you are very reasonable and forgiving and take time to listen to others who may have done you wrong. You are not one to hold grudges and harbor ill feelings toward others. You do not even think of exacting revenge on those people who cross you.

Boars are highly regarded for their chivalry; with your good heart, you readily sacrifice your own well-being for the greater good. Your self-avowed mission is to help others, and regardless of some unwanted circumstances, you do not back off, but barrel on with the hope that everything will turn out well in the end.

Your strengths, including your warmth and honesty, lead you to a satisfying life. Once you start a relationship or any undertaking, you pursue it, even if it takes a long time to achieve the expected results.

DOMINANT STRENGTHS	DOMINANT WEAKNESSES
Helpful	Vengeful
Well-mannered	Naive
Warmhearted	Sluggish
Even-tempered	Too trusting
Loyal	Passive
Honest	Conservative
Gentle	Stubborn
Forgiving	Emotional

豬

PERCEIVED WEAKNESSES

You are prone to being overly trusting. Although you might enjoy participating in serious talks, you are often perceived to be slow and shallow. When things do not go the way you want them to, you easily become disappointed. You may give in to your quick temper and, pushed too far, you do not hesitate to show your ferocious side.

You can be a little too laid-back and naive—so much so that other people may use your passive nature to take advantage of your natural kindness. Despite being manipulated, you still believe that everyone is inherently good. You need to be more assertive and refrain from allowing yourself to be the object of other people's wicked machinations. Being hopelessly optimistic, however, you do not always listen when advised to be less trusting. You do not like trouble, so are easily pacified after a conflict situation.

Your lack of competitive spirit but propensity for material pleasures make you stray into an uncertain future. This could lead to you making bad choices and decisions in life which, in extreme cases, could cause mental health issues or anxiety disorders.

PROSPECTS FOR YOUR CAREER

A hard worker, you are well liked for your dependability and honesty. You may try various jobs in your early years, but feel most fulfilled when helping others. You are highly regarded by your colleagues and employers and are willing to give up your time for the greater benefit. You have a great sense of humor, and because you enjoy making people happy, you can be an excellent host, entertainer, politician, or social advocate.

ROLE IN THE WORKPLACE

Despite a tendency to hog the spotlight, you always show your character strengths in the workplace. You are popular and can be very loyal to your company or organization. You are fearless and utterly dedicated to your work. Highly diligent and calm, you are averse to competition. You are also very patient and understanding; when people make mistakes, it is not such a big issue for you. You prefer to help fix the situation because you want the best for everyone. These qualities make you suitable for jobs in teaching and public service.

CAREER PROSPECTS

You may pick up several causes as your sense of involvement is strong. Your passion for community work makes you an excellent fundraiser for the charities you support. Charity work suits you because you are a selfless individual who wants to be of help to those in need. Your goal in life seems to be for everyone to live in harmony. Jobs that involve financial management may not be good for you. Also, if you decide to go into business, you need to be very discerning. You may take risks, but only carefully calculated ones.

You are happiest when you are learning new things. It seems that no matter what career you choose, you have great chances for success. Although you generally possess good wealth luck, you need to be mindful of how you manage your own finances, because you can be negligent in this area. At times, your negligence can get the better of you, but if you are able to find a job where your potential and talents have room to grow, you are bound to see great achievements.

PROSPECTS FOR DOMESTIC LIFE

Typically easygoing and amiable, you love to have people around you—you are a born entertainer. You want an easy life, devoid of complications, but may easily give in to temptations, especially those of the epicurean kind. Your love for luxury foods and drinks could make you gain weight. This is fine, as long as you remain active and see the value of proper exercise.

HOME STYLE

A yin water animal, your place of residence has an eclectic feel to it. You likely have a variety of your lucky colors: brown, yellow, and gray, alongside plenty of wood and metal features. The water energy features in decorative fountains or artwork depicting water or the winter season. Above all, your home reflects your nature as a highly sociable and party person. You love to relax and want family members and house guests to be as comfortable as possible. Plush lounge chairs are a hallmark of your interior design. Lighting is moderate, not too bright and rooms are generally free of too much electronic or technology-related gadgets. Instead, you prefer to display your personal sources of pride—trophies, medals, and similar citations for stellar achievements.

FAMILY

You symbolize patience and kindness, both highly evident in your role as a parent. You are very protective and always there for your offspring—although you are gentle and peace-loving, you can be aggressive if you feel you need to protect your children from harm. You act more like a friend than a disciplinarian, and there is such trust between you and your young ones that there are rarely any secrets kept. While this trait is admirable, you must take care lest you find other people, including their children, taking advantage of your kindness to serve their own interests.

Naturally happy, you attract other people to you with your gift of gab. You use your engaging style to keep your children entertained. With your keen imagination, you can hold the attention of young people, who will sit for hours listening to your stories.

FRIENDSHIP AND LOVE

Gentle and affectionate, you are devoted to family and make a great love partner. You truly value romance. Once you convince yourself that you have found the one, you do everything to show your love, showering your intended with sweet, and sometimes expensive, gifts. You may even use your sense of humor to attract the object of your affection. You have no qualms showing your interest in someone and do not stop until you know how you can continue to be in touch with that person. You turn on the charm by engaging in funny but meaningful conversations.

PARTNERSHIPS

In terms of friendship, you are most compatible with those born in the years of the Rabbit, the Sheep, and fellow Boars. The courageous Tiger provides the security you need—the Tiger is your secret friend—while you have much in common with the quiet Rabbit. Outside of these ideal partnerships, you can also enjoy harmonious relationships with the Rat, the Dragon, the Ox, the Horse, the Rooster, and the Dog, all of whom have characters that contribute to a workable union.

Relationships with those born in the years of the Snake and the Monkey are full of tension, however. Your warmhearted honesty is at odds with the suspicious and guarded nature of the Snake. And the Monkey is simply too mischievous.

ROMANCE

You tend to have an old-fashioned view on love, which makes others see you as slow; in truth, you are sensitive and mild-mannered. It could be that you are too restrained about revealing your feelings and tend to wait a long time before declaring your intentions. Indeed, these qualities—whether real or mere perceptions—can lead to you missing that chance of making your true feelings known.

You are quite an emotional type, but others are slow to notice when you are feeling down. You are sensitive but are not the type to complain easily. One quality you have that can hurt a relationship is your being too honest. If your partner commits a mistake, you find it hard to forgive and may say truly hurtful words. Overly sensitive, you may find yourself having many quarrels.

FRIENDS AND ALLIES

RABBIT   SHEEP   BOAR

THE PERFECT MATCH — TIGER

CELEBRATING

CHINESE

NEW

YEAR

Chinese New Year (CNY), also known as Lunar New Year or Spring Festival, is the grandest and most important annual event for the Chinese. With more than four thousand years of history, it is celebrated not only in mainland China, but also in many of China's neighboring countries, and even in Western countries where there are Chinese communities.

CNY PREPARATIONS As early as one month prior to the festival, the Chinese get busy buying gifts, decorations, food, and new clothes. They give doors and windows—important entryways of luck—a new coat of paint and clean their houses in the belief that getting rid of clutter is like letting go of stale luck and makes room for new and positive energy to come in. Every nook and cranny, cupboard, and refrigerator is rid of unwanted items.

As part of the clear-out, people make necessary repairs, especially on anything that leaks because this indicates money loss. People fill their rice bins to the brim, stocking them with enough rice to last the entire fifteen days of the festival. By the eighth day before CNY, people make sure their annual feng shui cures and enhancers are in place. Finally, they hang red paper strips as decorations. On them, they write different wishes for a happy life, continuous prosperity, and good health.

FESTIVAL MUST-HAVES

In most households, occupants fill vases with fresh flowers to signify spring and growth. They place oranges and tangerines—popular symbols of happiness—on plates, along with eight kinds of dried fruits. The pomegranate is also included, because of its red color, which is believed to drive evil spirits away. Its many seeds symbolize fertility. People prepare red packets containing "lucky money" as gifts. This gesture of giving is believed to bring good luck to both the giver and receiver.

FOOD FOR GOOD LUCK

Foods served during the festival are chosen for the type of luck they symbolize. Foremost is fish, which is usually served whole, because it represents abundance and having enough to share with others. For the same reason, chicken is also served in one whole piece for prosperity. Fishballs, meatballs, and rice cakes symbolize reunion and family closeness, perhaps because of their sticky nature. Noodles represent long life, and therefore must not be cut.

The guideline in food preparation seems to be "the more, the merrier," as a huge quantity of food represents abundance. At the very least, there should be eight types of foods on the table, including sweet desserts and fresh fruits that symbolize prosperity. The more vibrant the food colors, the better. Red, orange, green, and gold are believed to be lucky colors to have on the table. White, however, is considered unlucky; thus, tofu is avoided during these celebrations.

BELIEFS AND TRADITIONS

Here are some of the more popular beliefs and traditions surrounding the Chinese New Year.

Do not borrow and do not lend money. Doing so means the person doing the borrowing will likely owe money for most days of the year. Debts must be paid before New Year's Day.

Caution should be taken not to break anything as this could symbolize a failing relationship.

Avoid using bad language, unlucky words, or those with negative connotations such as "death," "killing," and "sickness."

Telling ghost stories is totally taboo at this time.

On New Year's Day, washing your hair or cleaning your house should be avoided. It signifies the washing or sweeping away of good luck.

Eating porridge is frowned upon because it symbolizes poverty.

Keep sharp objects out of sight for they represent quarrels and misunderstanding.

Crying on New Year's Day indicates a sad year ahead. Children are spared from scolding lest they cry and attract unhappiness and misfortune for the rest of the year.

On the stroke of midnight on New Year's Eve, doors and windows must be opened to allow the old year to go out and to let the new energies in.

The use of firecrackers on New Year's Eve is the Chinese way of sending out the old year and welcoming the New Year.

The Dragon Dance is usually performed to attract peace and prosperity. This important symbol of Chinese culture has become common in many countries of the world.

CHINESE NEW YEAR PRACTICES

The festival lasts for fifteen days from Chinese New Year's Eve to the Lantern Festival on the fifteenth day of the Lunar New Year. Practices observed at the start of a Lunar New Year are believed to influence events in the coming year.

DAY 1

Everyone rises early and dresses in their New Year's clothes to visit friends and relatives. They visit temples to offer incense and pray for a safe and prosperous year. Children and employees receive gifts in red packets. Slaughtering animals and eating meat are avoided.

DAY 2

Traditionally, married women return home to visit their parents, along with their husbands, after celebrating New Year's Eve with their in-laws.

DAY 3

It is inauspicious to do any house visiting, because evil spirits roam the Earth on this day and it is bad luck to be outdoors. The air is filled with the potential for possible disagreements among family and friends, so it is best spent at home.

DAY 4

It is believed that heavenly spirits such as the Kitchen God visit Earth on the fourth day, so it is considered auspicious to prepare a feast and make offerings of incense, food, and spirit money to welcome these deities and ensure a prosperous year ahead.

DAY 5

The so-called Festival of Po Wu is celebrated, to welcome the god of wealth. People open their doors and windows, burn incense, and set off firecrackers and fireworks to attract money, luck, and many forms of blessings. Local businesses reopen.

DAY 6

This is the day to discard old clothes, clean out the garage, and throw out trash around the house. These things are done to drive away the ghost of poverty and to give way for a better life during the New Year.

DAY 7

A celebration of Man's Day, the creation of mankind. Chinese people eat different healthy foods symbolizing abundance, prosperity, and long life. These include raw fish to promote success and noodles for longevity. The day is marked by reflecting on blessings and respect for all human beings.

DAY 8

A celebration of rice, the most essential Chinese staple food. Children are taught the importance of agriculture and where their food comes from.

DAY 9

A celebration of the birthday of the Jade Emperor, the supreme deity of Taoism. Food offerings and live chicken sacrifices are made in his honor.

DAYS 10-12

More visits among family and friends see plenty of feasting, drinking, and sharing happy moments with them.

DAY 13

This day is for cleansing and detoxing bodies that have been filled with rich food on the previous days. To help cleanse the digestive systems, vegetarian dishes are served on this day.

DAY 14

This is the day before the Lantern Festival. People prepare colorful lanterns and food. Dragon and lion dance teams practice for the big event.

DAY 15

The traditional Chinese Lantern Festival ends the Chinese New Year celebration. Streets and houses are decorated with lanterns and fireworks are set off. There is much public singing and dancing. Sticky rice balls called *tang yuan*, again to symbolize family cohesiveness, are the common fare in Chinese homes on this day. The day is a celebration of the birthday of Tian Guan, the Taoist "ruler of heaven," who is responsible for providing good fortune and wealth. Tian Guan is believed to like all types of entertainment, thus various kinds of activities are made in his honor to attract auspiciousness.

INDEX

RESOURCES

1. Lo, Raymond. *Feng Shui and Destiny*, Gardners Books (1992)

2. Lo, Raymond. *Feng Shui Essentials*, Feng Shui Lo (2005)

3. Lo, Raymond. *The Four Pillars of Destiny (Understanding Your Fate and Fortune)*, Times Books (1995)

ABOUT THE AUTHOR

MARITES ALLEN is an internationally recognized Feng Shui master and Chinese astrology expert who has trained with various masters from Malaysia, Singapore, Thailand, and China. She is the first Filipina to be awarded the prestigious title of "Master in Feng Shui" by the International Feng Shui Association in 2013. Marites has been an international Feng Shui consultant for more than twenty years, and has frequently appeared in global press, radio, and TV, including *This Morning*, the *Sun*, the *Express*, and CNN. She lives in London with her family and splits her time between the United Kingdom and Southeast Asia. You can visit Marites' website at maritesallen.com

First published in Great Britain in 2023 by Greenfinch,
an imprint of Quercus Editions Ltd., an Hachette UK company

First published in the United States in 2023 by

MandalaEarth

MANDALA

An Imprint of Insight Editions
PO Box 3088
San Rafael, CA 94912
www.MandalaEarth.com

Find us on Facebook: www.facebook.com/MandalaEarth
Follow us on Twitter: @MandalaEarth

ISBN 979-8-88674-030-1

10 9 8 7 6 5 4 3 2 1

Design and illustrations by Evi-O.Studio | Susan Le,
Wilson Leung, Katherine Zhang & Emi Chiba.

Printed and bound in China by 1010 Printing

MIX
Paper | Supporting
responsible forestry
FSC® C016973

Papers used by Greenfinch are from
well-managed forests and other responsible sources.